**Simon Vinnic**

# Cradle M

**Methuen Drama**

Published by Methuen Drama 2008

1 3 5 7 9 10 8 6 4 2

Methuen Drama
A & C Black Publishers Limited
36 Soho Square
London W1D 3QY
www.acblack.com

ISBN 978 1 408 11233 5

A CIP catalogue record for this book is available
from the British Library

Typeset by Country Setting, Kingsdown, Kent
Printed and bound in Great Britain by
CPI Cox & Wyman, Reading, RG1 8EX

**finborough**theatre

[ **finborough**playwrights season ]

# CRADLE ME

by Simon Vinnicombe

First performance at the Finborough Theatre, London:
Wednesday, October 1st 2008

# CRADLE ME

by Simon Vinnicombe

Cast in order of appearance

| | |
|---|---|
| Marion | **Sharon Maughan** |
| Daniel | **Luke Treadaway** |
| Louise | **Sarah Bedi** |
| Graham | **Paul Herzberg** |

Epsom, Surrey. The present.

Directed by **Duncan Macmillan**
Designed by **Paul Burgess**
Produced by **Shane Allin** and **Andrew Wall** for **SAW Productions**
Press Representative **Sue Hyman Associates**
Production Photography by **Daniel Link** danlink@hotmail.co.uk

The performance lasts approximately ninety minutes.

There will be one interval of fifteen minutes.

Our patrons are respectfully reminded that, in this intimate theatre, any noise such as rustling programmes, talking or the ringing of mobile phones may distract the actors and your fellow audience-members.

Interval drinks may be ordered in advance from the bar.

**Sarah Bedi** Louise

At the Finborough Theatre, Sarah appeared in *The Lady's Not For Burning*.
Trained at the Bristol Old Vic Theatre School. Other Theatre includes *Hamlet* (The Factory), *I Am A Superhero* (Theatre 503 and the Old Vic), *Romeo and Juliet* (Sprite), *Invisible Mountains* (National Theatre), and *The Late Middle Classes* (Watford Palace Theatre).
Television includes *Affinity*, *Casualty*, *Holby City*, *The Bill*, and *Doctors*.

Radio includes *One Chord Wonders*, *Parallel Lines*, *Beast At Bay*, and *Caring*.

**Paul Herzberg** Graham

Theatre includes *I.D.* (Almeida Theatre), *A Streetcar Named Desire* (Mermaid Theatre), *Dancing At Lughnasa* (National Theatre of Ireland – Abbey Theatre, Dublin), *The Dead Wait*, *Arms and the Man*, *Romeo and Juliet*, *While The Sun Shines*, and *People Are Living There* (Royal Exchange Theatre, Manchester), *The Merchant of Venice*, and *Carrington* (Chichester), *Julius Caesar* (Riverside Studios), *Goodbye Kiss* (Orange Tree Theatre, Richmond), *Oleanna* (Stephen Joseph Theatre, Scarborough) and *Pride and Prejudice* (Richmond).

Television includes *The Life and Loves of A She-Devil*, *Warburg*, *Smiley's People*, *The Knock*, *Poirot*, *Soldier Soldier*, *Napoleon and Josephine*, *Murder City*, *Band of Brothers*, *Dark Secret*, and *Seaton's Aunt*.
Film includes *Cry Freedom*, *The Dirty Dozen: Next Mission*, *Blood*, *Room 36*, *The Book Of Eve*, and *Almost Heaven* (which he also co-wrote).
Writing includes *The Dead Wait* which was shortlisted for the Verity Bargate Award, performed at the Market Theatre, Johannesburg, and at the Royal Exchange Theatre, Manchester where it won a *Manchester Evening News* Award for Best Actor, and was nominated for Best Play and Production; and *The Song Of My Father* (BBC Radio 4). He is currently writing *The Fighting Prince*, a screenplay for Focus Features, New York.

**Sharon Maughan** Marion

Trained at RADA.

Theatre includes *Habeas Corpus* (Lyric Theatre), *Filumena,* directed by Franco Zeffirelli (Lyric Theatre), *Plenty* (Liverpool Playhouse), *Born Yesterday* (Crucible Theatre, Sheffield), *Adam Was A Gardener* and *A Doll's House* (the Minerva Theatre, Chichester), *Arcadia* (National Theatre), and *All The Children Cried* (West Yorkshire Playhouse and New End Theatre, Hampstead) as well as repertory seasons at Chester and the Liverpool Playhouse. Sharon has also appeared in *Out of Our Fathers House* (Fountainhead Theatre, Hollywood, where she received a Drama Logue Award for Best Actress), and directed *Widowers Houses* (Chelsea Centre Theatre).

Television includes *Shabby Tiger, Dial M For Murder, The Main Chance, The Enigma Files, Keats, The Flame Trees of Thika, Dombey and Son, By The Sword Divided, Inspector Morse, Hannay, The Ruth Rendell Mysteries, Murder She Wrote, Felicity, Cinderella, Holby City* and *Twelfth Night* for which she was also Executive Producer. She was also seen on the long running series of commercials for Gold Blend coffee in the UK from 1987–1991, and in the USA from 1991–1998.

Film includes *Home Before Midnight, Another Stakeout, The Bank Job, and She's Out of My League.*

Writing includes the screenplay *Cross Country.*

**Luke Treadaway** Daniel

Trained at LAMDA.

Theatre includes *Saint Joan* and *War Horse* (both at the National Theatre) and *Piranha Heights* (Soho Theatre).

Television includes *The Innocence Project* (BBC), *Clapham Junction* (Channel 4).

Film includes *Northern Star, Heartless,* written and directed by Philip Ridley and co-starring Jim Sturgess and Timothy Spall, and playing a conjoined twin with his identical twin brother, Harry in the feature film *Brothers Of The Head* which won the prestigious Michael Powell Award for Best British Feature at the Edinburgh International Film Festival, and earned Luke a British Independent Film Award nomination for Most Promising Newcomer.

**Simon Vinnicombe** Playwright

Simon Vinnicombe's first play, *Year Ten,* received its world premiere at the Finborough Theatre in 2005 before transferring to the BAC in February 2006 as part of the *Time Out* Critics' Choice festival. The play has subsequently been produced across Europe and is now currently in development as a feature film to be produced by the First Film Company. Simon has also written *Turf* (Bush Theatre) and a radio play *Hard Road* (BBC Radio 4).

**Duncan Macmillan** Director

Duncan trained as a director at the Central School of Speech and Drama. Best known as a playwright, he is the winner of two Bruntwood Awards at the Royal Exchange Theatre, Manchester, is a member of the Royal Court/BBC 50 and the Old Vic New Voices and is the Pearson Writer in Residence at Paines Plough. As a founding member of the writers collective *the Apathists,* he has curated and directed evenings of new work at several London theatres totalling more than a hundred short plays, and is currently programming the autumn season of *Later* for Paines Plough at Trafalgar Studios. His plays include *Monster* (Royal Exchange Theatre, Manchester, and Manchester International Festival – nominated for Best New Play at TMA and MEN Awards), *The Most Humane Way to Kill A Lobster* (Theatre 503), *Satellite* (Young Writers Festival Readings at the Royal Court), and *I Wish To Apologise For My Part In The Apocalypse* (BBC Radio).

**Paul Burgess** Designer

Trained at Motley Theatre Design Course, following a degree in English at Oxford University. Designs include *On the Rocks* (Hampstead Theatre), *The Only Girl in the World* (Arcola Theatre), *Triptych* (Southwark Playhouse), *Jonah and Otto* (Royal Exchange Theatre, Manchester), *Black Stuff* (National Tour), *School of Dark* (National Tour and Unicorn Theatre), *Tom Fool* (Glasgow Citizens and Bush Theatre), *Much Ado About Nothing* (Shakespeare's Globe), *Babel Junction* (Hackney Empire), *Other Hands, Shoreditch Madonna* and *Flush* (all Soho Theatre), *Switch ECHO* (WUK, Vienna), *For One Night Only* (National Tour), *The Most Humane Way to Kill A Lobster* and *Cancer Time* (both Theatre 503), *Party Time/One for the Road* (BAC), *Peer Gynt* (Arcola Theatre), *Have I None* (Southwark Playhouse), *Sherlock Holmes* (La Tea, New York), *Women and Criminals* (Here, New York) and *Fred and Madge* (Oxford Playhouse). As a Director-Designer, he led devising on *Selfish* (The Arches, Glasgow, and Camden People's Theatre), *Out of Nothing* (The Junction, Cambridge) and *Rang* (National College of Arts, Pakistan, where he also led a seminar on scenography). As co-founder of Scale Project, he also collaborated on a programme of experimental work across the UK and in Siberia.

## SAW Productions

SAW Productions were founded in 2005 by Shane Allin and Andrew Wall to discover and develop new writing and to produce revivals of modern contemporary classics. Previous productions include the London premiere of *Visiting Mr. Green* by Jeff Baron at the New End Theatre, Hampstead, in March 2005, *Lady Day at Emerson's Bar and Grill* by Lanie Robertson at the New Player's Theatre in July 2005 and the world premiere of Stephen Berkoff's *Sit And Shiver* at the New End Theatre in May 2006 in association with the New End Theatre. The play enjoyed a sell out run before transferring to the Hackney Empire in January 2007. For further information, please visit www.sawproductions.co.uk

# **finborough**theatre

Finborough Theatre, 118 Finborough Road, London SW10 9ED
www.finboroughtheatre.co.uk | www.finboroughtheatre.co.uk

Artistic Director – Neil McPherson
Resident Designer – Alex Marker
Associate Director – Kate Wasserberg
Playwrights-in-Residence – James Graham, Peter Oswald, Al Smith, Laura Wade, Alexandra Wood
Literary Manager – Jane Fallowfield
Resident Casting Director – Rachel Payant
Development Producer – Rachael Williams
Resident Assistant Directors – Ben Kidd and Titas Halder
The Finborough Theatre is grateful for the support of The Invicta Trust

Smoking is not permitted in the auditorium and the use of cameras and recording equipment is strictly prohibited.

In accordance with the requirements of the Royal Borough of Kensington and Chelsea: 1. The public may leave at the end of the performance by all doors and such doors must at that time be kept open. 2. All gangways, corridors, staircases and external passageways intended for exit shall be left entirely free from obstruction whether permanent or temporary. 3. Persons shall not be permitted to stand or sit in any of the gangways intercepting the seating or to sit in any of the other gangways.

The Finborough Theatre is licensed by the Royal Borough of Kensington and Chelsea to The Steam Industry. The Steam Industry is under the Artistic Direction of Phil Willmott. www.philwillmott.co.uk The Steam Industry is a company limited by guarantee. Registered in England no. 3448268. Registered Charity no. 1071304. Registered Office: 118 Finborough Road, London SW10 9ED.

# **finborough**theatre

The multi-award-winning Finborough Theatre led by Artistic Director Neil McPherson presents new writing from the UK and overseas, Music Theatre and rediscoveries of forgotten work from the 19th and 20th centuries.

Founded in 1980, artists working at the theatre in its first decade included Rory Bremner, Clive Barker, Kathy Burke, Nica Burns, Ken Campbell and Clare Dowie. In the early 1990s, the theatre was at the forefront of new writing with Naomi Wallace's first play *The War Boys*; Rachel Weisz in David Farr's *Neville Southall's Washbag* which later became the award-winning West End play, *Elton John's Glasses*; and three plays by Anthony Neilson - *The Year of the Family*, *Normal* and *Penetrator*, which went on to play at the Royal Court. From 1994, the theatre was run by The Steam Industry. Highlights included new plays by Tony Marchant, David Eldridge, Mark Ravenhill and Phil Willmott, new writing development including Mark Ravenhill's *Shopping and F\*\*\*king* (Royal Court, West End and Broadway) and Naomi Wallace's *Slaughter City* (Royal Shakespeare Company), the UK premiere of David Mamet's *The Woods*, and Anthony Neilson's *The Censor*, which transferred to the Royal Court.

Since 2000, New British plays have included Laura Wade's London debut with her adaptation of W.H. Davies' *Young Emma*, and James Graham's *Eden's Empire* (both commissioned specially for the Finborough Theatre); Simon Vinnicombe's *Year 10* which went on to play at BAC's *Time Out* Critics' Choice Season; James Graham's *Albert's Boy* with Victor Spinetti; Joy Wilkinson's *Fair* which transferred to the West End, Nicholas de Jongh's *Plague Over England* with Jasper Britton, David Burt and Nichola McAuliffe; and Stewart Permutt's *Many Roads to Paradise* with Miriam Karlin. London premieres have included Sonja Linden's *I Have Before Me a Remarkable Document Given to Me by a Young Lady from Rwanda*; and Jack Thorne's *Fanny and Faggot* which also transferred to the West End.

UK premieres of foreign plays have included Brad Fraser's *Wolfboy*; Lanford Wilson's *Sympathetic Magic*; Larry Kramer's *The Destiny of Me*; Tennessee Williams' *Something Cloudy; Something Clear*; Frank McGuinness' *Gates of Gold* with William Gaunt and the late John Bennett in his last stage role (which also transferred to the West End); *Hortensia and the Museum of Dreams* with Linda Bassett; *Blackwater Angel* – the UK debut of Irish playwright Jim Nolan – with Sean Campion; and the English premiere of Robert McLellan's Scots language classic, *Jamie the Saxt*.

Rediscoveries of neglected work have included the first London revivals of Rolf Hochhuth's *Soldiers*, and *The Representative*; both parts of Keith Dewhurst's *Lark Rise to Candleford* – performed in promenade and in repertoire; *The Women's War* – an evening of original suffragette plays; *Etta Jenks* with Clarke Peters and Daniela Nardini; *The Gigli Concert* with Niall Buggy and Paul McGann; *Loyalties* by John Galsworthy; Noël Coward's first play, *The Rat Trap*; T.W. Robertson's *Ours*; Charles Wood's *Jingo* with Susannah Harker; and the sell-out production of Patrick Hamilton's *Hangover Square*.

Music Theatre has included the new (premieres from the UK and USA by Grant Olding, Charles Miller, Michael John LaChuisa, Adam Guettel and Andrew Lippa) and the old (the sell-out Celebrating British Music Theatre series reviving forgotten British musicals).

The Finborough Theatre was the only unfunded theatre to be awarded the prestigious Pearson Playwriting Award bursary for Chris Lee in 2000, Laura Wade in 2005, James Graham in 2006 and Al Smith in 2007 – as well as the Pearson Award for Best Play for Laura Wade in 2005 and James Graham in 2007. The Finborough Theatre also won the Empty Space Peter Brook Mark Marvin Award in 2004, and was the inaugural winner of the Empty Space Peter Brook Award's Dan Crawford Pub Theatre Award in 2005.

You can read more about at the theatre at
**www.finboroughtheatre.co.uk**

# Cradle Me

This play is for my grandparents,
Edith 'Bubbles' Vinnicombe
and Wallace Vinnicombe

## Characters

**Marion**, *forty-eight*
**Dan**, *seventeen*
**Louise**, *twelve*
**Graham**, *fifty-one*

The scene changes are integral to the action of the play and should not be hidden in blackouts or covered by music.

There should not be an emphasis on creating a reality in terms either of costume, set or lighting used in the piece.

\* An asterisk indicates a leap in time.

## Acknowledgements

I owe a huge debt of gratitude to Rachel Wagstaff, Duncan Macmillan, Nick Quinn and Sam Adamson for their generosity and support during the writing of this play. A big thank-you to Anthea Williams, Josie Rourke and all those involved in the Bush Theatre's 'Halo' project and to Andy and Shane at SAW. Special thanks to my friends Jody, Linky, Matt and his new son Joshua Elmes. I could not do anything without Roger, Julie, Steve, Tom and Susie Vinnicombe or Tracy: thank you for everything and much, much more.

Simon Vinnicombe, 2008

## Part One

**Marion** *is folding clean washing from a basket. She is taking some napkins from the pile and making four places on the dinner table. She folds the washing as she goes, placing the clothes on a chair. The clothes are clearly those of her two children and her husband.* **Dan** *enters hurriedly.* **Marion** *looks at him and smiles. This is clearly everyday.* **Dan** *begins to pace the room, trying to recover his breath.*

**Marion**   Why you out of breath?

**Dan**   –

**Marion**   Look at the state of you. You run everywhere, don't you? Do you want a towel?

**Dan**   No – no – no –

**Marion**   I'll get you one.

*She hands him a tea towel from the washing.*

Use this. He's not here, I don't think.

*She moves to off.*

Nicholas? Nicholas! I thought he went out with you. Do you want a drink?

**Dan**   Mrs Neill –

**Marion**   Cut that out. You don't fool me, you know. Not Mrs anything. You call me Marion.

**Dan**   Sorry. I –

**Marion**   I wish I ran everywhere like you. Wouldn't have such a tummy.

**Dan**   You don't have a tum— Mrs –

**Marion**   I was a size eight for twenty-five years, you know . . . You've got all the chat, haven't you?

**Dan** *nods.*

**Marion**    I was going to put his dinner on. Do you want some, Daniel?

**Dan**    I'm – I'm all right.

**Marion**    Your chest is still going. Look at you. Probably on the fags like that naughty bugger. My fault. I should never have had a drag in front of him, but sometimes you . . . It's terrible for you.

**Dan**    Yeah.

**Marion**    Have you been doing any practising for your exams?

*She exits for some more clothes.*

**Dan** (*distracted*)    A bit – bit, yeah.

**Marion** (*from off*)    Tell the truth now, won't you? Cos I'm worried about Nick. I don't think he is. He gets frustrated and – I think he gives up. Is he doing any practising?

**Dan** (*frustrated*)    I – I don't know, Mrs – Marion.

**Marion**    I don't know whether to punish him or not. Could nick that bloody record player off him or – but then he'll just sulk or – I worry he just listens to music and stops talking to people . . . There's so much to be had at your age, Dan. Girls and . . . Don't worry. I won't start. Are you going to wait for him?

**Dan**    There's been – I need you to – I need you t—

**Marion**    What, love?

**Marion** *re-enters.*

**Marion**    What's the matter?

**Dan**    I – He – I can –

**Marion**    Dan? Dan, love, what's the matter?

**Dan** *shakes his head, retreats from her.*

**Marion**    Dan? Dan?

**Dan** *shakes his head.*

**Marion**   Dan?

**Dan**   No.

**Marion**   Look, calm down now.

**Dan** (*still shaking his head*)   I won't. I can't.

**Marion** (*scared*)   You can't what, love?

**Dan**   I –

**Marion**   What is it?

**Dan**   I'm sorry –

**Marion**   What have you done?

**Dan**   I'm sorry, Marion –

**Marion**   Dan?

**Dan**   I'm sorry. I'm sorry. I'm sorry. I'm sorry. I'm sorry. I'm sorry.

*He is weeping.*

**Marion**   Where's Nick, Dan? Where is he?

**Dan**   –

**Marion**   Dan, you're scaring me. I need you to tell me – Dan?

*She grabs his head.*

**Dan**   There's been an acc— He's – Nick . . .

*

*Lights fall black. As they rise* **Louise** *is bringing on a full-length mirror. It is an old-fashioned, two-way, wooden-rimmed mirror, on wheels.* **Marion** *enters in a dress. She looks into the mirror as* **Louise** *stands behind it in a bright pink dress doing her best not to be seen.* **Marion** *preens herself in the mirror.*

**Louise**   It's not black.

**Marion**   Doesn't have to be black.

**Louise**   I'll get changed. I don't want to stand out.

**Marion**   Love –

**Louise**   I don't want to go.

**Marion**   Lou –

**Louise** *shakes her head.*

**Marion**   Don't you think Nick would want you to be there, love?

**Louise**   I don't care.

**Marion**   Don't say that.

**Louise**   Did you hear him last night, Mum?

**Marion**   He's just a bit upset.

**Louise**   He was sat in the garden talking to himself.

**Marion**   Lou –

**Louise**   And walking around.

**Marion**   What?

**Louise**   He's not dressed yet, Mum –

**Marion**   Lou –

**Louise**   Sat there in his bloody pants.

**Marion**   That's your dad you're –

**Louise**   Is he going mad?

**Marion** (*stops her a bit*)   He'll come later.

**Louise**   Is he going to be all right?

**Marion**   I don't know, love.

**Louise**   Are you going mad, Mum?

**Marion**   Don't be daft.

*She rubs* **Louise**'s *hair, smooths it down onto her head. She stands her in front of the mirror, preens her.* **Louise** *does not flinch.*

*Silence.*

**Louise**    I don't want to sit in the front at the church, Mum. They'll be looking to see if I'm crying or not.

**Marion**    They won't, love.

**Louise**    They will. When we went to Billy Turner's funeral everyone was staring at her mum cos you could hear her sniffing and her husband was holding her up.

**Marion**    You didn't say.

**Louise**    She made a noise like a whale.

**Marion**    You don't have to sit at the front if you don't want to.

**Louise**    Can I sit with Dan?

**Marion**    I expect he'll be with his mum –

**Louise**    Will you cry, Mum?

**Marion**    I don't know.

**Louise**    Should I cry?

**Marion**    Lou –

**Louise**    What if I don't?

**Marion**    It's all right – it's all right not to –

**Louise**    Do they bury him in his clothes?

**Marion**    What?

**Louise**    When he goes into the ground in that bloody – Does he have clothes on?

**Marion**    I don't think you need to know that sort of thing, Lou.

**Louise**    I want to know. What will he be wearing?

**Marion**    I –

**Louise**   He won't be naked, will he?

**Marion**   No.

**Louise**   In the wooden –

**Marion**   Lou –

**Louise**   Does he have a pillow?

**Marion**   I –

**Louise**   He'll get cold if he's naked, won't he?

**Marion**   Love –

**Louise**   Why does everyone have to come to our house after?

**Marion**   They come to show their respect.

**Louise**   Fat bloody Janet is coming to fill her face –

**Marion**   That's your auntie –

**Louise**   Can I stay upstairs and not talk to anyone?

**Marion**   Be nice if you came and said hello.

**Louise**   I look like an idiot.

**Marion**   You're so pretty.

**Louise**   No, I'm not. My hair is frizzy and crap, my clothes are rubbish and I walk like a man.

**Marion** (*brushes* **Louise**'s *hair*)   You look lovely.

**Louise**   I fucking hate pink.

\*

**Louise** *quickly moves the mirror off and exits.* **Marion** *settles by the table. It's late, the evening of the funeral. She sits and clutches a tea towel. Drops the towel. She clutches her head and then covers her ears with the inside of her wrists as if hearing an awful sound. She falls forward from her chair. Covers her eyes as if blinded by the light. She buries her head.*

**Dan** *enters. For a moment he stands and watches* **Marion** *crouched over.*

**Dan** (*unsure whether or not to go to her*)  . . . Marion?

**Marion**   Sorry, love?

**Dan**   It was a nice service.

**Marion** (*distracted*)   Eh? (*Looks at* **Dan**.) Do you think so?

**Dan**   I liked it when Louise spoke. She's so . . .

**Marion**   What?

**Dan**   I couldn't do it.

**Marion**   It was when they put the soil on the coffin, the sound of the wet soil hitting the wood. I couldn't put soil on – I can't bury my . . . I wanted a white coffin. It's white coffins for children. Because he's seventeen, but – he's just a child, Dan. You're just children.

**Dan**   You did very well, Marion.

**Marion**   Apart from sobbing into the grass and – Got mud all over my new dress and everything.

**Dan**   I think you look lovely.

**Marion**   You are funny.

**Dan** (*embarrassed*)   Why?

**Marion**   Don't be embarrassed. It's . . . (*She smiles.*) That song you played was beautiful. What was that?

**Dan**   'Many Rivers to Cross'. Jimmy Cliff.

**Marion**   He liked that one?

**Dan**   Yeah.

**Marion**   Obsessed with his reggae – vinyl –

**Dan** (*half laugh*)   Yeah.

**Marion**   My fault, I used to collect – not reggae though. Too macho, all that – Supremes and Vandellas – Loved those . . .

**Dan** *smiles.*

**Marion**    Some Ronettes.

**Dan**    Yeah?

**Marion**    I haven't listened to music for . . .

**Dan**    You should.

**Marion**    I don't know why, love. You stop having hobbies – obsessions.

**Dan** *paces a little, uncomfortable, reaching for some words.* **Marion** *is in a world of her own.*

**Marion**    You don't realise when you're sat in the garden and Nick's running around like a lunatic and Louise and her mate are taking the piss out of you – and – and he's trying to make you laugh. You don't realise that this is it, 'these are the good times', you're too busy worrying about whether or not the sausages are burning and . . . Life casts such awful dark shadows.

**Dan** *nods. Stops still.*

*Long silence.*

**Marion**    Did Nick ever . . . Did . . . Did Nick ever . . . Did he ever have sex, Dan?

**Dan**    I . . . I dunno . . .

**Marion**    Dan?

**Dan** (*doesn't know how to answer this*)    I . . . er . . .

**Marion** (*a little desperate*)    I need to know – I need to. Did he? Did he?

**Dan**    Yes. Yes, Mrs Neill. Yeah, he did.

**Marion** (*nods*)    Good. Good. I'm glad of that. Good. Thanks, Dan. That's . . .

*Silence.*

Your mum says you've been getting nightmares.

**Dan** *nods.*

**Marion** (*tilts her head to the side childishly*)   Oh, love.

**Dan**   Can I still come round?

**Marion**   Of course you can. Louise likes you –

**Dan**   Wouldn't be weird?

**Marion**   We're all really fond of you.

**Dan**   But –

**Marion**   You're our neighbour, love.

**Dan**   Thank you.

**Marion**   There's so much food left –

**Dan**   Yeah.

**Marion**   Why don't you take some of the champagne to your mum?

**Dan**   She hardly drinks.

**Marion**   All the food they've left –

**Dan**   I dunno.

**Marion**   'Melon and Parma Ham'. That's his Aunt Janet, that is – pretentious cow.

**Dan**   I didn't like it.

**Marion**   The house was so full today.

**Dan**   Heaving –

**Marion**   They're all smiling – beacons of consolation and sympathy – and now it's . . .

**Dan**   I could come round.

**Marion**   I don't want it to be tomorrow morning.

**Dan**   I'll take Lou to school.

**Marion** (*smiles*)   You are good.

**Dan**   Nah, it's –

**Marion**    She'd love that. Thank you so much for today too –
Thank you for helping clear up and . . . Your mum will be
wondering where you got to.

*Silence.* **Dan** *fidgets a bit. Kicks his feet. Uncomfortable. Can't find the
words.*

**Dan** *(can't say it)*    I – I . . . I got really nervous in there. When
they brought out the coff— I kept wanting to shout something
out in the church, a rude word or something and –

**Marion**    Dan –

**Dan**    Is that wrong? And . . . and . . . and – I didn't know
what to do with the order of service because they've got a
picture of him on the front and – and . . . and I didn't want to
throw it away cos that's Nick – and – and – I can't throw Nick
away, can I?

*He pulls out the picture, he holds it tightly.*

**Marion**    It's all right, love, relax . . . (*She stands and moves to
him.*) You throw those pictures away. I've got plenty of pictures
of Nicholas . . . All right?

*She removes the picture from his clenched hand.* **Dan** *nods repeatedly,
trying to prevent the tears.*

**Marion**    Oh, love.

**Dan**    I'm all right – I'm all right – I'm all right.

**Marion**    I've got one thing more thing to ask of you, Daniel.

**Dan**    What's that?

**Marion**    I could do with a hug. Will you give me a hug?

**Dan** *moves to* **Marion***. They hold one another.* **Dan** *clings to*
**Marion** *tightly. His head is buried into her shoulder, he smells her dress.
She tries to look peer at his face, but he is still pressed against her. She
rocks him gently to comfort him. He does not let go for a time.*

\*

**Marion** *exits.* **Dan** *watches her leave, does not take his eyes off her.*
**Louise** *crosses her mother and grabs* **Dan**'s *arm and leads him away.*
*A swing unravels from above.* **Dan** *stands as* **Louise** *sits on the swing,*
*kicking her feet a little.*

**Louise**    You're only five years older than me.

**Dan**    Half a decade.

**Louise**    You're weird.

**Dan**    Why?

**Louise**    I saw you walking around last night outside.

**Dan**    Did you?

**Louise**    Were you looking for Nick?

**Dan**    I'm not mental.

**Louise**    People at school think you're weird, don't they?

**Dan**    No.

**Louise**    What's it like to be a geek?

**Dan**    Shut up.

**Louise**    Bit of a loner?

**Dan**    I'm not.

**Louise**    You could get some new friends?

**Dan** *doesn't respond. He pushes her on the swing. They say nothing for*
*a short time.*

**Louise**    I liked walking with you. Nick made me walk ten
yards in front when he took me to school.

**Dan**    Did he?

**Louise**    Have you got halirosis?

**Dan**    What's that?

**Louise**    One of the girls said you had smelly breath.

**Dan**    Who said that?

**Louise**   Sinead Fulton.

**Dan**   Who the fuck is –

**Louise**   I didn't say it –

**Dan**   It's halitosis anyway. Divvy bitch –

**Louise**   I didn't –

**Dan**   Not you. Her.

**Louise**   Hayley thinks you're fit, though.

**Dan** (*brightens a little*)   Really?

**Louise**   I know. Made me feel a bit sick.

*Silence. He stops pushing.*

Why are you stopping?

**Dan** *rolls his eyes, pushes her on the swing.*

**Louise**   Will you be walking me tomorrow?

**Dan**   Maybe.

**Louise**   Cos Hayley might walk with us tomorrow. I don't want you getting off with her.

**Dan**   Can't she walk on her own?

**Louise**   No. There's a flasher round her way. Been wanking off in front of the girls up by the pond.

**Dan**   What?

**Louise**   He's got a big dirty green mac and apparently he's got a huge one.

**Dan**   Louise –

**Louise**   Looks like a baby python apparently.

**Dan**   Lou –

**Louise**   Hayley said it was a bit like a pig's leg. Can you imagine that?

**Dan**    Can we just –

**Louise**    Maybe we could hold hands?

**Dan**    I . . .

**Louise**    I'm only joking. Should have seen your face. You went all mental.

**Dan**    No I didn't.

**Louise**    Bloody beetroot. That means that I'm sexually advanced.

**Dan** (*laughs*)    You what?

**Louise**    That means that I'm flowering. Because if I was still a kid you wouldn't feel funny about holding hands, would you? But now it has romantic implications.

**Dan**    Stop it.

**Louise**    You might get a big stiffy.

**Dan**    Stop it –

**Louise**    A pig leg –

**Dan**    You're too young to be talking like –

**Louise**    Do you like coming to our house?

**Dan**    Yeah.

**Louise**    Even though he's not here any more?

**Dan**    I – (*He can't find the words.*)

**Louise**    I know you sneak in to play his records.

**Dan**    I haven't got one at home.

**Louise**    Get a CD player, you pikey.

**Dan**    It's not the same.

**Louise**    Such an old man.

**Dan**    Do you ever stop talking?

**Louise**    It's weird. Be smoking a pipe soon. Eating toffees.

**Dan**    Piss off.

**Louise**    I could be your friend.

**Dan**    Lou –

**Louise**    If you are a loner.

**Dan**    You're twelve.

**Louise**    So?

**Dan**    Sorry. I didn't mean –

**Louise**    I'm a young woman now.

**Dan** (*laughs*)    Bee-have.

**Louise**    Darren Feaney says he wants to finger me. Should I let him?

**Dan**    You what?

*He stops pushing her.*

**Louise**    Says I can wank him off if I do.

*Silence.*

Well . . . ?

**Dan**    No, you don't want to.

**Louise**    I bet you like being wanked off, don't you?

**Dan**    What do you know about it?

**Louise**    Don't be patronising. Hayley's had sex.

**Dan**    What!

**Louise**    She told me all about it.

**Dan**    Hayley?

**Louise**    I know more than you know.

**Dan**    She's twelve for fuck's sake.

**Louise**   Eleven. I'm three months older than her, actually.

**Dan**   Fucking hell.

**Louise**   She said it hurt. Does it really hurt?

**Dan**   Yes, it's bloody agony.

**Louise**   So shall I let Darren –

**Dan**   No.

*He continues pushing her.*

**Louise**   I don't like it at school at the moment. People look at me like I'm something in a museum. I'm 'the one whose brother died'. I don't want to be the one whose brother died.

**Dan**   I know.

**Louise**   I fucking hate the loony doctor as well –

**Dan**   Loony doctor?

**Louise**   I have to see Mrs Barnes every Tuesday. Bereave— Therapy things. Talk to her about all sorts of rubbish.

**Dan**   What like?

**Louise**   My dreams and . . . She's got a moustache.

**Dan**   Has she?

**Louise**   You miss him, don't you? . . . I know he's all right. Hayley reckons there ain't no such thing as angels but I know he has got his own angel and she is looking after him.

**Dan** *stops pushing her. Silence.*

**Louise**   Do you think there is such a thing as angels?

**Dan** (*firm*)   No.

**Louise**   Why aren't you pushing?

*He starts to push again.*

Is that one your bedroom? (*She points up.*)

**Dan**   Yeah.

**Louise**   I bet you watch loads of porn, don't you?

**Dan** (*half-laugh*)   Shut up.

**Louise**   Will you stay for dinner?

**Dan**   If your mum says it's all right.

*

**Dan** *walks away. After he exits,* **Louise** *continues to swing until* **Graham** *enters. They see one another. She runs past him and inside the house.* **Graham** *clings to the rope of the swing. Feels the rope. Puts it to his face. Bows his head. He pushes the swing gently, then kicks at it angrily. Sits slumped on the swing. He eats some chocolate.*

**Marion** *watches him, approaches him.*

**Marion**   Love?

**Graham** *looks up.*

**Marion**   You shouldn't, you know.

**Graham** *looks down at the chocolate.*

**Graham**   Leave it out.

**Marion**   No – not that. She can't see you like –

**Graham**   What?

**Marion**   You need to . . . hold on to yourself – for –

**Graham**   I'm fine.

**Marion**   Lou can see you from the kitchen.

**Graham**   Why isn't she in bed?

**Marion**   She won't go.

**Graham**   She's going to school tomorrow.

**Marion**   Leave her.

**Graham**   Why haven't you put her in bed?

**Marion**   She won't go.

**Graham**   I can't take her tomorrow.

**Marion**   Dan's going to.

**Graham**   Eh?

**Marion**   Dan's been walking her.

**Graham**   Right. Right.

**Marion**   OK?

**Graham**   She all right? Is she . . . ?

**Marion**   Hasn't blinked.

**Graham**   I'll be late tomorrow.

**Marion**   When will you . . . ?

**Graham**   I'll try and get back by nine. It's . . .

**Marion**   I know.

**Graham**   It's just bad timing.

**Marion** (*hurts*)   Yeah.

**Graham**   Another client dinner. Fucking hate taking them out.

**Marion**   Don't worry.

**Graham**   Might be like this for a bit.

**Marion**   How long?

**Graham** *stands to leave. Picks up the chocolate.*

**Graham**   We should go inside.

**Marion**   Yeah.

**Graham**   I was just thinking we could get rid of this (*swing*). Lou doesn't use it, does she?

**Marion**   We can't. She does. We can't.

**Graham**   He stopped years ago too.

**Marion**    I don't want to –

**Graham**    She's getting too old –

**Marion**    No.

**Graham**    Marion –

**Marion**    What?

**Graham** *goes to speak but doesn't. He stands. Wonders a little.*
**Marion** *watches him.*

**Graham**    I should have spoken, shouldn't I?

**Marion**    Love –

**Graham**    At the service –

**Marion**    I –

**Graham**    Why didn't I speak?

**Marion**    It's hard to –

**Graham**    It's eating me, you know?

**Marion** *cannot offer a response.*

**Graham** (*getting worked up*)    I can't carry on . . . like this,
Marion.

**Marion**    –

**Graham**    I'm going in.

**Graham** *leaves. The swing is hauled up.*

\*

**Marion** *moves towards the table. She sits.* **Dan** *enters with a bottle
of wine and a glass. He opens the bottle and hands* **Marion** *a glass of
wine. He takes pleasure in pouring it for her.*

**Marion**    Louise has decided she doesn't like spaghetti
bolognese now. Telling me she wants to be a bloody
vegetarian.

**Dan**    I couldn't live without meat.

**Marion**    If she wants any of that tofu nonsense she can cook it herself.

*Silence.* **Dan** *watches her prepare the food.*

**Dan**    I've got one of Nick's jumpers at the house.

**Marion**    Which one?

**Dan**    Grey Adidas one – with the rip in it.

**Marion**    You keep it.

**Dan**    You sure?

**Marion**    Keep it, love.

**Dan**    If you need anything doing around the house I could do it for you?

**Marion**    I think we're all right. Thanks though, love.

**Dan**    I could mow the lawn.

**Marion**    Not sure I can afford you, Dan.

**Dan**    I wouldn't want you to pay me. It would be my pleasure.

**Marion**    Haven't you got anywhere else you'd rather be?

**Dan**    Nah.

**Marion**    Really?

**Dan**    Get a bit bored after school, to tell the truth.

**Marion**    Don't you have any other friends at college?

**Dan**    No.

**Marion**    But surely you must want to –

**Dan**    I don't go out all that much – never really gone much further than Ewell. There's got to be more to life than Surrey, hasn't there?

**Marion**    You'd bloody hope so. Do you go into London much?

**Dan**   No, I think it's shit.

**Marion**   Really?

**Dan**   In my head it's incredible – like something in a film, all nightclubs and beautiful women. You spend the whole time walking around looking for a place that someone says they knew and you never find it – and you end up in some shitty place called something like the Zoo Bar in Leicester Square, and it's shitty, really shitty, and all the men are angry and the women harassed. It's just like Epsom but bigger and uglier. It's shit.

**Marion** (*laughs*)   You are funny.

**Dan**   Am I?

*Silence.*

**Marion**   Why are you looking at me like that?

**Dan**   I'm wondering how you're doing?

**Marion**   I'm all right. (*She smiles.*) It's nice to be asked.

**Dan**   Can I help with the dinner?

**Marion**   You could lay the table.

**Dan**   Is it just you and me?

**Marion**   And Lou. I'll leave his in some foil.

**Dan** *begins laying the table.*

**Louise** *enters.*

**Louise**   Is it ready yet?

**Marion**   No.

**Louise**   Mum, Dan's got halitosis.

**Dan**   No I haven't.

**Marion**   Leave him alone, love.

**Louise**   He wants to get off with Hayley.

**Marion**   Lou –

**Louise**   I know. It's disgusting.

**Marion**   Lou –

**Dan** (*to* **Marion**, *embarrassed*)   I would never –

**Marion** (*smiles*)   Ignore this one. She likes to wind people up.

**Louise**   He's gone purple again. Look at him.

**Marion**   Leave him alone.

**Louise**   I'm only joking.

**Marion**   Well, stop it.

**Louise**   There's a bloke been going round interfering with himself in front of the first years at school.

**Marion**   Are you making things up?

**Louise**   No. Tell her, Dan. Isn't there a flasher?

**Dan**   There's a rumour.

**Louise**   Not a rumour. You're such an arse-kisser, you are.

**Marion**   Louise. Don't talk like that.

**Louise**   'There's a rumour.' He's trying to be all mature again. Sound like you've got a peach stuck in your mouth.

**Marion**   Leave him alone.

**Louise**   It is true though. Hayley saw him.

**Marion**   Oh, Hayley. Then it must be true.

**Louise**   She's not a liar, Mum.

**Marion**   No, love, she's just creative.

**Louise**   Whatever.

**Dan**   When you've got a minute, Marion, I'd –

**Louise** (*teasing*)   What do you want, Daniel?

**Dan**   Like a word with your mu—

**Louise** (*mimics*)  'When you've got a minute.' What do you sound like?

**Marion**  Lou. What is it, love?

**Dan**  Don't matter.

**Marion**  Would you like to stay, Dan? I'm doing a roast chicken.

**Louise**  Mum . . . meat!

**Marion**  You'll eat it and you'll enjoy it, cheeky.

**Louise**  It's bloody minging though.

**Marion**  Don't swear, you.

**Louise**  'Bloody' is in the dictionary, Mum. So's 'bastard' and 'shit'. So they must be all right, mustn't they?

**Marion**  Not in this house.

**Louise**  You say 'shit' when you drop something in the kitchen. You whisper it but I can hear you.

**Marion**  Haven't you got some homework to be doing?

**Louise**  No.

**Marion**  You had German today, he always gives you some homework.

**Louise**  I'm terribly fatigued today.

**Marion**  Get.

**Louise**  I bet he's got some homework.

**Dan**  Had free periods all afternoon.

**Louise**  I want to be in the sixth form. You do fuck-all work.

**Marion**  Louise!

**Louise**  I've got to go and do my homework now, Mum.

*She exits.*

**Marion**  She's a one, isn't she?

**Dan**   Yeah.

**Marion**   Shall I put some wine in the chicken?

**Dan**   That would be nice.

**Marion**   I might do some exercise, you know. I'm getting so big. Could cut down on the booze.

**Dan**   I don't think you need to.

**Marion**   I've got a muffin top as well. That's what Louise calls it.

**Dan**   A muffin top?

**Marion** (*points to her love handles*)   Bit above your hips, all spilling over . . . I was thinking about doing some of that Pilates stuff. They do it at the leisure centre. Doesn't your mum go?

**Dan**   Yeah. Yoga . . . all that. She's a bit obsessed.

**Marion**   I put it on in a blink these days. It's so depressing. You need to be able to look at yourself in the nude without being disgusted. I think that's pretty important.

**Dan**   Are you working at the pub tonight?

**Marion**   No, they've been good since . . . I'm going to go back to three evenings a week I think. I'll try and find something a bit more . . .

**Dan**   Do you like it?

**Marion**   I'm forty-eight, Dan. I don't like my job. Everyone looks at me like I'm piss on a wall. You're not allowed to be my age and work in a bar, are you? That means you've failed, doesn't it? The women take such pleasure in ordering me about and they never offer a thank-you when I serve them, and the men – the men feel like they have the option to do what they want with you. They look angry with you for being too old to look at and leer and then by half past ten they're all 'All right, darlin', fancy a bit of young stuff?' and all of a sudden they want to throw me over the bar and express their manhood. Every person I deal with seems to want to remind me of my failings.

**Dan**    They're the ones who've failed though, aren't they?

**Marion**    And they're all so confident. When did everyone get so confident?

**Dan**    I don't go in on the weekend, it's full of arseholes. Bored wankers. Fight night on Friday and Saturday. All the blokes who haven't pulled fighting in kebab shops. It's depraved.

**Marion**    Yes, it is. That is exactly the right word, Dan.

*Silence.*

What?

**Dan**    Nothing.

**Marion**    You look right through me, you do.

\*

**Graham** *is alone. He has two cardboard boxes and appears to be looking through them. He takes pieces from each box and throws them into a bin liner. He continues to do this with several items. He pulls a photo out of one of the boxes. He gazes at if for a long time. It is a picture of Nick as a toddler. He puts the picture into his pocket and carries the boxes off.*

\*

**Dan** *is pacing in front of* **Marion**. *She watches him as he appears to be struggling to say something. She smiles at his struggle.*

**Marion**    What is it, love?

**Dan**    I . . . I . . .

**Marion**    Yes?

**Dan**    I bought you something. I've been trying to . . . I –

**Marion**    Did you?

**Dan**    I wanted to.

**Marion**   You are sweet.

**Dan** (*suddenly*)   Can I come tomorrow?

**Marion**   Course you can.

**Dan**   I wanted to see you again. Tomorrow. Lunchtime.

**Marion**   Haven't you got work to do?

**Dan** (*shrugs*)   . . . Can I?

**Marion** (*smiles*)   I'm not going anywhere.

**Dan** (*pulls a small wooden box out of his pocket*)   Your present.
I made it, in fact. I make them myself. You put it on your
wrist. They're beads from the floor of the South American
rainforest, they are.

**Marion**   It's lovely, very colourful.

**Dan**   Do you like it?

**Marion**   I don't want to touch it, my hands are all wet. Will
you put it on for me?

**Dan**   You don't have to wear it just for me.

**Marion**   Put it on, I love it.

*She holds out her wrist. He puts the bracelet on with real care.*

I've been getting dreams too, Dan.

**Dan**   Yeah?

**Marion**   A nightmare . . . I hear a sound. A dreadful noise
that presses down on my skull. All the while it's getting darker
and darker until this light blasts through and sort of . . . blinds
me. It's like one of them dreams where you try and force your
eyes open. I heard it at the grave – Horrible, Daniel.

*She holds her wrist up into the light. She kisses the top of* **Dan**'s *head.*

**Marion** (*the bracelet*)   It's beautiful.

**Dan**   I've written you a letter.

**Marion** (*smiles*)   Have you?

**Dan**    There are certain things I want to say to you. Things that I want to . . . and I have it right in my head but when it comes to saying it I get all . . . and I can't say it. I want what I say to be true.

**Marion** (*slightly confused*)    Right.

**Dan**    So I wrote it. In a letter.

*He hands* **Marion** *the letter.*

**Dan**    I'd like it if you read it when I'm not here.

**Marion**    OK, love.

**Dan**    Goodnight then.

**Marion**    Dan?

**Dan**    Yes.

**Marion**    You're all right, aren't you?

**Dan** (*smiles*)    Yeah. Yes, I am.

**Marion**    I'm glad you come and see me.

\*

**Dan** *exits hurriedly.* **Marion** *sits. After a short time* **Graham** *enters clutching a bundle of clothes.*

**Graham**    Do you want any of these?

*She doesn't respond. He drops the clothes on the floor.*

I said do you want any of these?

**Marion**    Stop it.

**Graham**    Stop what?

**Marion**    Just . . .

**Graham**    Is there anything you want to keep?

**Marion**    Why are you being so cruel?

**Graham**    I'm not. I'm . . . we need to . . .

**Marion**   Just take them. Do what you want with them.

**Graham**   I'm going to paint it –

**Marion**   What?

**Graham**   The room needs a paint.

**Marion**   No.

**Graham**   There's a smell –

**Marion**   A smell –

**Graham**   A sound, then –

**Marion**   Can't we just –

**Graham**   What?

**Marion**   Wait.

**Graham**   You look nice today . . .

**Marion**   Graham?

**Graham**   I'll get some paint . . . I'll . . . I'll . . .

*She looks to him to say more. He exhales. He moves to her. Holds her. He wraps his arms around her but* **Marion***'s body remains limp. He kisses the top of her head.*

**Graham**   I should . . . crack on.

**Marion**   Yeah.

\*

**Louise** *is standing in front of the large mirror. She changes her top. She takes out some make-up and begins to put some eyeliner on. She is not well practised at this and she struggles. She then tries to put lipstick on. She does not like this and quickly wipes it off. She works on her eyes a little more, some eyeshadow. She stands back from the mirror and blinks a little. She adjusts her clothes and looks at herself sideways on. She smiles into the mirror. She takes the mirror off.*

\*

**Dan** *enters with a large tablecloth. He spreads it across the table with the help of* **Marion**. *They look across the table at one another as they do this.*

**Dan**    What time does he get back?

**Marion**    Keeps coming back late –

**Dan**    Will he be home soon?

**Marion**    Why are you asking about –

**Dan**    Is Lou asleep?

**Marion**    I doubt it. You know what she's like.

*Silence.*

(*Half embarrassed.*) What are you looking at?

**Dan**    Did you ever – in the summer – sometimes – when you were outside, I –

**Marion**    I've seen you watching me.

**Dan**    You . . .

**Marion**    When I was in the garden and the sun was out. I used to have my bikini top on. You used to look at me out of your window, didn't you?

**Dan**    I . . .

**Marion**    I saw the curtains twitching.

**Dan**    Did you mind?

**Marion**    All part of growing up, I suppose.

**Dan**    I said did you mind?

**Marion** *looks away, embarrassed.*

*Silence.*

**Dan**    I'm not a child. I do know about sex, you know.

**Marion** (*a little patronising*)    What do you know?

**Dan**    I know where you stick it in, Mrs – Marion.

**Marion**   Do you?

**Dan**   Yeah.

**Marion**   What about what a woman wants?

**Dan**   Yeah.

**Marion** (*half-laugh*)   Yeah? Do you know how to pleasure a woman?

**Dan**   I've read stuff. I've seen some stuff.

**Marion**   Not porn, I hope. Always look like they're trying to harm the woman in those films. Frightened, angry men who don't like women. That's my Graham's problem. He thinks my wincing and muffled groans mean he's doing well.

**Dan** *laughs a little.*

**Marion**   Men do need vocal encouragement, I suppose.

**Dan**   No, I don't think like that. I . . . I wouldn't be like that.

**Marion** (*laughs*)   Really? I did have a good lover. A boy before Graham, when I was sixteen. They say the first time's supposed to be horrible, but it was . . . Felt like our bodies melted into one another, it was beautiful.

**Dan**   I heard that – I reckon it's – it's like that Otis Redding song, 'Try A Little Tenderness', it starts off like really gentle, slow and sort of soft and . . . tender, I suppose, and then it starts to move a bit and sort of build gradually and gradually, it keeps on building more and more until this sort of – euphoric – sort of . . . climax.

**Marion**   Where did you hear that?

**Dan**   Some woman on the telly talking about her first . . . you know?

**Marion**   You are a strange one.

**Dan** (*hurt*)   Why?

**Marion**   Do you have a girlfriend, Dan? At college?

**Dan** (*shakes his head*)   No.

**Marion**   You should. 'S good for you.

**Dan**   I don't like them.

**Marion** (*laughs a little*)   Why?

**Dan** *shrugs.*

**Marion**   You were always with him, weren't you . . . ?

*Silence.*

**Dan**   Your necklace looks nice.

**Marion**   Thank you.

**Dan**   It's all right.

**Marion**   Goodnight, Dan.

**Dan**   Is it time?

**Marion**   It's late.

**Dan**   I don't want to go to sleep.

**Marion**   Why, love?

**Dan**   I just – (*He can't say it.*) Sleeping . . . Sometimes I can't –

**Marion**   Nor me –

**Dan**   Don't want to sleep.

**Marion**   He turns out the light and I can't close my eyes.

**Dan**   I have his music. I listen. I am with him . . . I have that – I . . . I'm not on my own.

**Marion**   No –

**Dan**   I'm not –

**Marion**   Is that why you walk Lou?

**Dan**   No – no – I want to help – want to be of help. I . . .

*

**Dan** *has an armful of records. He handles them with extreme care. He walks to the table and plugs in the record player. He sifts through them and holds up a record to the light. He places the record on the player and uses a cloth to clean it meticulously. He then places the sleeve back in the cover, takes the needle and places it on the record. He sits in a chair and listens attentively while reading the lyrics from the sleeve. The song, 'It Must Be True' by Toots and the Maytals, plays for a time before* **Graham** *enters. He stands behind* **Dan** *and watches him. He looks as if he has been sleeping and carries a carton of juice. He watches* **Dan** *for some time. His face softens as he watches him, and he waits until the record begins to fade before speaking.*

**Graham**   Hello, mate.

**Dan** *is startled. Turns the music off.*

**Dan**   Jesus – you –

**Graham**   She's not in, is she?

**Dan**   Who?

**Graham**   Marion. Did a bunk today. Don't want her to –

**Dan**   Not back yet –

**Graham**   Tired.

**Dan**   I didn't mean to just walk in –

**Graham**   'S all right. Always used to.

**Dan**   Yeah.

**Graham**   We like to see you.

**Dan**   Yeah?

**Graham**   I know it might not seem like it since . . .

**Dan**   No.

**Graham**   But we do.

**Dan** *(makes a move to leave)*   I'm –

**Graham**   You're all right, mate. Sit down.

**Dan**  Sorry.

**Graham**  Want some juice?

*He holds up the carton, wipes the mouth of the carton with his sleeve.*

**Dan**  I'm –

**Graham**  Here.

*He hands **Dan** the juice. Sits at the table. Looks at record cover.*

**Graham**  What you got?

**Dan**  It's Nick's record. Marion said it was –

**Graham**  It's all right. Relax, mate. What is it?

**Dan**  Toots and the Maytals.

**Graham**  Oh yeah. Reggae. Not really my . . . Is she coming back soon, do you know?

**Dan**  Half an hour, probably.

**Graham**  I should get dressed.

**Dan**  Work?

**Graham**  On lates this week. It's busy – at work –

**Dan**  I heard.

**Graham**  I should be here. I know –

**Dan**  It's none of my –

**Graham** (*looking around*)  These walls have been speaking. I fucking swear it.

*Silence. **Graham** stands. He looks at **Dan**. He looks at the record.*

**Graham**  He liked them, did he?

**Dan** (*nods*)  His favourite.

**Graham**  Right.

**Dan**  More than Dekker or the Melodians. Jimmy Cliff comes close but – Toots. Fucking legends. Sorry. (*Swearing*)

**Graham** (*laughing a little*)    You are a funny one.

**Dan**    Some Marcia Griffiths too, but – I prefer the blokes.

**Graham**    Right. I didn't really know he . . . Not my –

**Dan**    Yeah.

**Graham**    How's school?

**Dan**    It's . . . (*Shakes his head.*)

**Graham**    I thought school was shit. Forced to hang around with people you don't like. Fucking bullied. Fucking bored. Fucking scared. Fucking shit.

**Dan**    Yeah.

**Graham** *looks at him and laughs a little.* **Dan** *laughs too.*

**Graham**    Any nice girls?

**Dan** (*shakes his head*)    No.

**Graham**    It's the best time for all that, you know? Girls. So fucking exciting at your age. You should sleep with as many as you can, not just that . . .

**Dan**    Right.

**Graham**    You should get stuck in – to everything . . .

**Dan**    Right.

**Graham** (*sees* **Dan**'s *discomfort, smiles*)    You like listening to your music, don't you?

**Dan**    Yeah.

**Graham**    Put that on again, will you?

**Dan** *puts the needle on the record. The song continues for some time.* **Graham** *is watching* **Dan** *as it plays. He looks away. Reaches across suddenly and stops the music.*

**Graham**    I should – I should get to work . . . So . . .

**Dan** (*understands, collects the records*)    OK.

**Graham** (*stops him*)   Wait. Can I?

*He takes the Toots record from* **Dan**.

**Graham**   You don't mind?

**Dan**   No. Course – they're . . .

**Graham** *exits with the record.* **Dan** *runs off with the rest of the records.*

\*

*The swing is lowered as* **Graham** *exits.* **Marion** *stands in the garden.* **Dan** *enters, breathless.*

**Marion**   I wondered if you'd come today.

**Dan** *breathes hard.*

**Marion**   What is it?

**Dan**   Where were you yesterday?

**Marion**   I –

**Dan** (*firm*)   Where were you?

**Marion**   What's the matter, love?

**Dan**   I came. You weren't here.

**Marion**   When? I was out. What's the matter, love?

*He looks at her, still breathing heavily.*

Did you jump over the fence? Didn't hear you.

*He continues to look at her.*

**Marion**   What's that face for?

**Dan**   Did you read it?

**Marion**   What are you talking about?

**Dan**   My letter.

**Marion**   No, love, I meant to –

**Dan** (*getting worked up*)   I – I –

**Marion**   I've had so many letters to respond to . . . I –

**Dan** *nods.*

**Marion** (*softly*)   I'm sorry. I'll read it now, shall I?

*There is a silence.* **Marion** *is searching* **Dan**'s *face, trying to understand what is wrong. He steadies himself, speaks with real urgency, his eyes never leaving* **Marion**. *He speaks, as if from memory.*

**Dan**   I'd open up my heart for you. I'd hand it to you and say do with it what you will. I'd do anything you wanted at any time. Be there for you. Hold you. Help you. Cradle you. I could love you in a way you never believed possible. Because I think that you're extraordinary. You elevate me. I want to tear out my heart and carve the word . . . Everything about you screams the word 'beautiful'. I like the way you look down and I lose your eye contact for a second and you – you look back up and I'm knocked out by just how beautiful you are all over again. I like the way you walk, you've got a bit of the tomboy in you and you bounce around with such enthusiasm for everything. So open and just perfect . . . You read it, Marion. You read what I wrote to you . . . Believe me, Marion. I could make you so happy. He doesn't deserve you. You don't deserve it. Let me love you. Cos I don't care if you break my heart – I'm willing to take that chance – I'll take that risk – cos I want to be with you more than you can possibly imagine. Marion . . . Marion . . . Marion.

**Marion**   Dan –

**Dan** (*shaking*)   Don't you say it!

**Marion**   Graham is –

**Dan**   He's not here. I know he's not here. Don't you –

**Marion**   Dan –

**Dan**   I know you feel the same.

**Marion** *laughs.*

**Dan**   Why are you laughing?

**Marion**   I didn't mean to –

**Dan**   You held me.

**Marion** (*stunned*)   What?!

**Dan**   I know that you're feeling it too.

**Marion**   What are you talking about –

**Dan**   Look at me!

**Marion**   Dan –

**Dan**   I know it!

**Marion**   Daniel – I'm sorry –

**Dan**   Don't say it!

**Marion**   I think you may have misunderstood me –

**Dan** (*shaking, on the verge of tears*)   You don't know what you're talking about –

**Marion**   I don't mean to hurt you –

**Dan** (*tries to block out what she is saying, shakes his head*)   No –

**Marion**   Dan –

**Dan**   No – no – no –

**Marion**   Love –

**Dan**   I know you – I know that you feel . . .

**Marion**   I'm sorry –

**Dan**   Don't say it! Don't you dare say it!

*She moves towards him to comfort him.* **Dan** *pushes her away. She is shocked.* **Marion** *looks at him. She turns and leaves.*

\*

**Louise** *enters with the tablecloth from the table.* **Dan** *follows her. They sit on the cloth. The swing remains lowered.* **Louise** *wears the top she wore in front of the mirror.* **Dan** *looks distraught.*

**Louise**   You're not paying attention.

**Dan** (*distracted*)   Eh?

**Louise**   What's up?

**Dan**   What?

**Louise**   You're not paying attention –

**Dan**   I am.

**Louise**   You're not.

**Dan**   Lou –

**Louise**   Look at me –

**Dan** (*annoyed*)   Fuck's sake.

**Louise**   Dan?

**Dan**   What!

**Louise** (*soft*)   I nicked you a beer.

**Dan**   Where did you get that?

**Louise** (*smiles, proudly*)   From the cupboard.

**Dan**   He'll do his nut.

**Louise** *opens the beer and drinks some defiantly.*

**Dan**   Lou.

**Louise**   Tastes like shit.

**Dan**   Don't drink that.

**Louise**   How long before I'm pissed?

**Dan**   Stop it.

**Louise** *stands and begins to twirl round and round.*

**Louise**   Hayley says if you spin round you get off your chunk quicker.

**Dan**   Sit down.

**Louise**   She said –

**Dan**   Are you wearing make-up?

**Louise** (*guiltily*)   No.

**Dan**   Lou –

**Louise**   I'm not.

**Dan**   Why isn't your dad at work?

**Louise**   I got in trouble.

**Dan**   Why?

**Louise** (*shrugs*)   Do you like our groundsheet?

**Dan**   Eh?

**Louise**   We could camp out, couldn't we?

**Dan**   You what?

**Louise**   Sleep out here.

**Dan**   No.

**Louise**   Why not?

**Dan**   Cos.

**Louise**   It'd be a laugh.

**Dan**   They won't fight for long.

**Louise**   They will. This is serious.

**Dan**   Why?

**Louise**   Dunno.

**Dan**   Lou . . . ?

**Louise** (*almost proudly*)   I got suspended today.

**Dan**   Eh?

**Louise**   I hit Kirsty Bingham. Made her bleed. And cry.

**Dan**  Why?

**Louise** *bows her head.*

**Dan**  Lou?

*She drinks determinedly.*

What's the matter?

*She shakes her head.*

Lou?

*She begins to cry a little.*

It's all right, Lou.

**Louise**  I can't.

**Dan**  You can't what?

**Louise**  I don't want to cry.

**Dan**  You're allowed.

**Louise**  I don't want to!

**Dan** *goes to her. She moves away.*

**Louise**  She said Nick . . . She heard Nick's head came off when they crashed the car.

**Dan**  Jesus.

**Louise**  Did his head fall off, Dan?

**Dan**  No, Lou.

**Louise**  You did see the car?

**Dan** (*nods*)  I ran to your mum.

**Louise**  Why didn't you stay with him?

**Dan**  I was frightened.

**Louise**  Were you?

**Dan**  I don't want to talk about it –

**Louise**    Please?

**Dan**    What do you want?

**Louise**    Just want to know what he looked like –

**Dan**    You know what he looked like.

**Louise**    That's not what I mean –

**Dan** (*frustrated*)    Just –

**Louise**    Why don't you hang around school any more?

**Dan** (*unsettled*)    I dunno.

**Louise**    You always used to be round by the park with Nick n' that.

**Dan**    So?

**Louise**    You could still go out.

**Dan**    I've got exams.

**Louise**    Really?

**Dan**    I don't want to go.

**Louise**    Why?

**Dan**    Other kids are – They're fucking stupid. Vain. Boring. They're all . . . fucking –

**Louise**    Bloody hell –

**Dan**    Fucking wannabe bad boys, fucking make-up, fucking orange skin, fucking pointless fucking –

**Louise**    Is that why you're always round my house?

**Dan**    I have to walk you home.

**Louise**    Saw you sneaking out the garden when I got back from gymnastics.

**Dan**    I was helping your mum with something.

**Louise**    Why you always helping her?

**Dan**    She's had a tough time, Louise.

**Louise**   I've had a tough time too.

*Silence.*

Would you ever go with a girl from Year 8?

**Dan**   Like Hayley?

**Louise**   No.

**Dan**   Look, Lou –

**Louise**   Why wouldn't you?

**Dan**   I didn't say I wouldn't, I just –

**Louise**   Would you dry my face for me?

**Dan**   Yeah.

*He goes to her.*

**Louise**   No. Would you do it with your hands?

*He takes her face in his hands and wipes her face gently.*

**Marion** *enters. She sees* **Dan** *wiping* **Louise***'s face.* **Dan** *sees her and steps back.* **Louise** *turns to face her mum.*

**Louise** (*firmly*)   What?

**Marion**   Is everything all right?

**Louise** (*annoyed*)   Yeah. Why shouldn't it be?

**Marion**   Have you been –

**Louise**   What do you want, Mum?

**Marion** *looks concerned. She looks to* **Dan***, who looks away, then to* **Louise***, who is growing more agitated by her presence.*

**Marion**   Your tea will be ready soon.

**Louise**   Fine.

**Marion**   Are you all right, Daniel?

*He nods, does not make eye contact.*

Right. Well, I'll . . .

**Louise**    Bye, Mum.

**Marion**    Five minutes, Lou.

**Louise** *waits until* **Marion** *has gone.*

**Louise**    She's such a weirdo sometimes.

**Dan**    Parents.

**Louise**    Do you fancy my mum?

**Dan**    What?

**Louise**    Do you?

**Dan**    Don't be ridiculous . . . No, that's . . . No.

**Louise**    That would be disgusting.

**Dan**    Are you really all right?

*He kisses her on the cheek.*

**Louise**    I might change my bedroom.

**Dan**    Really?

**Louise**    I think it's a bit girly. Do you think it's girly?

**Dan**    I dunno . . .

**Louise**    What should I have on my walls? What have you got?

**Dan**    I've got Jimmy, Toots, Rhyging and Dekker.

**Louise**    I don't like reggae. I think it sounds like the CD got
a bit stuck.

**Dan**    You just don't understand.

**Louise**    I don't like it.

**Dan**    Who do you like?

**Louise**    I quite like Vivaldi, *Four Seasons.*

**Dan**    Really?

**Louise**    No . . . dickhead. (*She laughs.*)

**Dan**    You've got to stop hanging around with Hayley.

**Louise**  She's gone off you now. Says your hair makes you look too effeminate.

**Dan**  Right.

**Louise**  If it hurts if a boy's got a big dick, then why is it so important that a boy has a big one?

**Dan**  Why do you want to know that?

**Louise**  I don't get it.

**Dan**  Never you mind.

**Louise**  Have you got a big dick? I bet you're hung like a hamster. You could show me if you want?

**Dan**  What?

**Louise**  I'm only joking.

*

**Dan** *picks up the tablecloth. They exit.* **Marion** *enters after a time as the lights dim. She wears a nightdress and a dressing gown. Holds her slippers in her hand. She goes to the window. She looks out.* **Graham** *enters behind her. He is in a dressing gown, which is open. He is wearing boxer shorts and a T-shirt.*

**Graham**  Are you coming to bed?

**Marion**  In a minute.

**Graham**  What are you doing there?

**Marion**  Looking at the garden.

**Graham**  I'll do the lawn when I get time, I promise.

**Marion**  Dan said he'd do it.

**Graham**  What does he want for it?

**Marion**  Said he'd do it for nothing.

**Graham**  He's a good boy.

*Silence.*

Come to bed.

**Marion**   I'm restless.

**Graham**   I made an effort to be here.

**Marion**   I know.

**Graham**   So we could go to bed at the same time.

**Marion**   I'm sorry.

**Graham**   I'm sorry I haven't . . .

**Marion**   What?

**Graham**   Been here.

**Marion**   I understand. Work.

**Graham**   Yes – work.

**Marion**   It's all right.

**Graham**   It's not, though. I've been . . . I haven't . . .

**Marion**   It's fine, love.

**Graham**   I will be . . . better.

*Silence.*

Am I too fat?

**Marion**   You what?

**Graham** (*half-laugh*)   Have I let myself go?

**Marion**   No. I like the way you look, love.

**Graham**   I'm worried I might have . . .

**Marion**   No.

**Graham**   Would you come to bed?

**Marion**   I think I might watch some telly. You get to bed.

**Graham**   Marion?

**Marion**   I won't be long. I'm . . .

**Graham**   Are you crying?

**Marion**   No, love. I'm fine.

**Graham**   Talk to me, Marion.

**Marion**   Really, I'm –

**Graham**   I'm not fine, love. I'm not!

**Marion**   Graham –

**Graham** (*speaks over the top of her*)   I know that in about three hours –

**Marion**   Love –

**Graham** (*louder*)   I'll be having that same nightmare.

**Marion**   Could you –

**Graham**   I used to get one where he was playing with matches. Wake up terrified and –

**Marion**   Don't –

**Graham**   I'll get a glimpse of him in his car and I'll be next to him. I can talk to him, I can tell him to . . . I can protect him, do what a dad's –

**Marion**   Graham, love?

**Graham**   Yeah?

**Marion**   It's . . . you must sleep, love. You're doing yourself no good.

**Graham**   I thought if we spoke . . . I thought that maybe you're feeling what I'm . . . I thought – I thought –

**Marion**   I'll be up soon.

**Graham**   Come to bed.

**Marion**   I won't be long, love.

*

*They look at one another.* **Graham** *exits, exasperated.* **Marion** *ties her dressing gown and puts on her slippers. A light appears on* **Dan** *who is sitting against the wall of his bedroom. He has a blanket draped over his legs and appears to be rolling a spliff. He has a portable stereo next to him, playing 'Monkey Man' by Toots and the Maytals. There are several vinyl records piled next to him. One of the sleeves is open, the lyrics to the music are on the page. As* **Marion** *enters his space he makes a hurried and clumsy attempt to hide the spliff under the blanket.*

**Marion**   I told your mum I had to ask you something.

**Dan**   Oh.

**Marion**   She gets in such a tizz. Thinks I'm going to have a breakdown in front of her or –

**Dan**   She likes you.

**Marion**   Must look like a basket case in my slippers.

**Dan** *half laughs.* **Marion** *laughs with him. She stops herself, makes a shushing gesture with her finger to her lips and points downstairs to indicate that* **Dan**'s *mother is down there.*

**Marion**   I can't sleep.

**Dan**   Nor me.

**Marion**   You've got a nice bedroom.

**Dan**   Thanks.

**Marion**   Nice posters. I wish I still had posters. You take your character and throw it all over the walls when you're younger, don't you? Still finding out who you are. I should do that, you know? Get to my age and you just have inane rubbish all over the walls, stuff you think might make you look interesting to other people . . . Silly, really.

*Silence.*

**Dan**   You've been crying.

**Marion**   Stinks of Lynx in here.

**Dan**   I was having a smoke. Don't want my mum to –

**Marion** (*giggles*)   Can I have some?

**Dan** *gets out a metal box with Rizla etc. and begins to roll a joint.*

**Dan**    Are you sure?

**Marion**    I have smoked weed before, you know.

**Dan**    Really?

**Marion**    Haven't had any for years, though. I used to like it. Made me go all sleepy. Marvellous on a hangover.

**Dan**    Yeah.

**Marion**    Don't do it too often, though, will you? You'll end up a boring person if you do it too much.

**Dan**    Feel my triceps.

*She blurts out a laugh.*

**Marion**    Do what?

**Dan**    Don't laugh. Go on.

**Marion** *does.*

**Marion**    They're very –

**Dan**    I'm sorry about . . . I'm sorry that . . .

**Marion**    It's fine, love. It's forgotten.

**Dan**    I'm sorry, I couldn't help –

**Marion**    Don't.

*Silence. She sees the record sleeve on the floor.*

What record is that?

**Dan**    Toots.

**Marion**    You read the lyrics?

**Dan**    Course.

**Marion**    Do you know them by heart?

**Dan**    Course. The words are everything.

**Marion** (*smiles*)    Why reggae?

**Dan**   He showed me what the songs mean. It's not discovered like all that other stuff. People should have known more about Toots, Dekker, Jimmy Cliff. Bob Marley is worshipped by people but he doesn't have the heart of Toots. Might as well listen to bloody Aswad.

**Marion** (*smiles*)   Is that right?

**Dan**   I don't like any of the electric sounds of the more modern stuff. They taint it.

**Marion**   Right.

**Dan**   I like it cos it's how you feel without any of the rubbish that gets in the way.

**Marion**   That's nice.

**Dan**   Is the smell bad? Shall I open the window?

**Marion** (*smiles*)   No.

**Dan**   Do you want a pillow or . . . ?

**Marion**   I'm fine.

**Dan** *stands.*

**Dan**   I could get you one –

**Marion**   I'm fine.

**Dan**   If you need one?

**Marion**   Sit down.

**Dan** *sits. They don't speak for some time.*

**Dan**   What do you want to talk about?

**Marion**   Don't want to talk about anything.

*She takes his hand.*

**Dan**   Oh.

*He gazes down to look at their hands linked together. The music plays louder.*

## Part Two

*Dan enters the kitchen of **Marion**'s home with a bag for college. He begins laying a place at the table for **Louise**. **Marion** enters and watches him. She brushes his arm with her hand by way of a thank-you. **Louise** enters with **Graham**. **Graham** goes to **Marion** and tentatively places his hand on the small of her back. He kisses the back of her head. He is eating a piece of toast.*

**Graham**  Morning, love. (*To **Dan**.*) Morning, mate.

**Marion** *offers **Dan** a spare slice of toast. He shakes his head, begins repacking his school bag. **Graham** pulls out a chair on which **Louise** sits. He begins brushing her hair. **Marion** sits and drinks some juice.*

**Louise**  Dan's been working out, Mum. He wants to be a Muscle Mary.

**Marion**  Leave him alone, Louise.

**Louise**  Feel his guns though. They're getting big.

**Marion**  Guns?

**Louise**  His arms, Mum. That's what the muscle boys call their arms.

**Dan**  Leave it out.

**Louise**  I'll come for a run with you if you like. I won cross-country by three bloody minutes, I did.

**Marion**  Don't swear, you.

*Silence.*

**Louise**  Can we play a game?

**Marion**  Lou –

**Louise**  I know a really good one. Not rude.

**Marion**  Eat your food.

**Louise** (*her hair*)  Ow!

**Graham**  You've got loads of knots.

**Louise**  No, I haven't.

**Graham**  You have.

**Louise**  I straightened it.

**Graham** (*hurts*)  What you doing that for?

**Louise**  Looks better.

**Graham**  But I like your hair.

**Marion**  Leave her.

**Graham**  She'll be plucking her eyebrows next.

**Louise** *looks at him guiltily.*

**Graham**  You're not –

**Louise**  Dad –

**Graham**  Bloody hell.

**Louise**  You're being embarrassing.

**Marion**  Leave her.

*Silence.*

**Louise**  Can we play a game?

**Marion**  Lou –

**Louise**  I've got a really good one –

**Marion**  Eat your food.

**Louise**  It's brilliant.

**Graham**  I'll give you two a lift if you like?

**Dan**  I –

**Louise**  No.

**Graham**  I'm sure Dan will let you sit in the front.

**Louise** (*embarrassed*)  Shut up, Dad.

**Graham**    What have I said?

**Louise**    I like walking.

**Louise** *gets up from chair, sits with* **Marion**.

**Graham** (*to* **Marion**)    What time did you come to bed?

**Marion**    I dunno. About three.

**Louise**    Did you have a nightmare?

**Graham**    You should've woken me.

**Marion**    You must sleep.

**Graham** (*wipes his mouth*)    Are you going to do our lawn, Dan?

**Dan**    If you want me to.

**Louise**    I could trim it. Use the strimmer machine.

**Marion**    No.

**Graham**    It's very good of you.

**Dan**    Not really –

**Graham**    Your mum must be really proud.

**Marion** (*to* **Graham**, *to stop him*)    Love –

**Graham**    She must be, though.

**Dan**    We'll be late, Lou.

**Graham** (*remembers, huge grin*)    Oh, Dan!

**Dan**    What?

**Graham**    That record is incredible.

**Marion**    What record?

**Graham**    It's blown my mind, mate.

**Marion**    What are you talking about?

**Graham**    'Bam Bam'. What a track that is.

**Marion**    You've been listening to . . . ?

**Graham**    I've got to have it for the car.

**Louise**    Can we go now, Dan?

**Graham**    I'll get it on CD.

**Dan** *makes a face at this.*

**Graham**    What did I say?

**Dan** (*disapproving*)    CD?

**Graham**    What?

**Dan** (*to* **Louise**)    Come on.

**Louise** (*toast*)    Can I bring this with me?

**Marion** *nods.*

**Louise** *exits, followed by* **Graham**. **Dan** *remains looking at* **Marion** *for a time. He pulls the tablecloth and all that's on it onto the floor. He removes his bag and jumper. He plays some music.* **Marion** *re-enters with a bottle of champagne in her hand. She dances a little to the music.*

*

*There are now two empty champagne bottles on the table. A CD plays quietly in the background. It is Toots and the Maytals, 'Sweet and Dandy'.*

**Dan**    That was disgusting.

**Marion**    Posh champagne, that was. You're not supposed to say it's disgusting. Nice bottle of Bolly.

**Dan**    I'd rather have a lager.

**Marion** *giggles*

**Dan** (*laughing a little*)    I've never seen you drunk before.

**Marion** (*laughs*)    How dare you! I'm not drunk. I'm just a bit happy.

**Dan**    You look great.

**Marion**    Feels really naughty having a drink in the day. We should tidy up –

**Dan**    Nah –

**Marion**    Graham will be home soon.

**Dan**    Leave it.

**Marion**    What?

**Dan**    We're not doing anything wrong.

**Marion** (*laughs*)    No, we're not.

**Dan**    We haven't done anything wrong.

**Marion**    No.

**Dan**    Haven't done anything.

**Marion**    What does that mean?

**Dan**    I love this song.

*He turns up the music. It is Toots and the Maytals' 'It's you'.*

Watch this.

You've got your football-bloke dance –

*He dances with an exaggerated air of cool.*

You've got your shit-football-players' dance –

*Dances badly.*

Your pissed-up-rugby bloke who's all 'birds and rah-rah', bunch-of-twats dance with their pelvis cos they got no dicks –

*Performs a clumsy dance leading with his pelvis.*

Your gay-man dance –

*Camp box-shaped dance.*

Feed the ducks –

*Moves his hands as if handing out birdseed.*

And of course your big fish, small fish –

*Dances as if marking out the shape of the fish as he goes.*

**Marion** *laughs as he mixes them all together.*

**Dan**    That's your Epsom nightlife for you right there.

*He turns the music down and catches his breath.* **Marion** *watches him giggling.*

**Marion**    I'm glad you're here.

*They giggle a little.*

I can feel the bubbles going through my legs.

**Dan**    Feels great.

*There is a sound off.*

What was that?

**Marion**    Just the wind – it's all right.

*They both keep still. Turn music off.*

**Dan**    What time is it?

**Marion**    You really should leave, love.

**Dan**    Yeah –

**Marion**    It doesn't look very –

**Dan**    Dance with me.

**Marion**    We can't. What if –

**Dan**    Come on.

**Marion**    Dan. Let's tidy up now.

**Dan** (*dances in front of her, charming*)    You look so beautiful, Marion. Dance with me.

**Marion** (*coyly*)    No.

**Dan**    Come on.

*He goes to stroke her face, but does not.*

**Marion**    You're naughty.

**Dan**    My head's spinning a bit.

**Marion**    You're not going to be sick, are you?

**Dan**    No.

*They giggle.*

**Marion**    It's time, love.

**Dan**    You don't want me to go.

**Marion**    You have to go.

**Dan**    Five more minutes –

**Marion**    Dan –

**Dan**    Then I promise I'll go.

**Marion**    Sit on the floor.

**Dan**    What?

**Marion**    Sit on the floor. I'll rub your hair. Feels lovely when the bubbles are going round.

**Dan** *sits beneath her as she strokes the hair on his head.*

**Dan**    Relaxing.

**Marion**    It's supposed to be.

**Dan**    Will you have a bath with me?

*He turns his head to look at her. She does not speak.*

*

*The swing is lowered.* **Marion** *begins hurriedly to clear the mess.* **Dan** *slowly puts his shoes back on and leaves.* **Marion** *exits quickly with empty bottles in her arms.* **Graham** *takes the bottle of champagne from the table and sits on the swing.* **Dan** *stands next to him.* **Graham** *is drunk, breathing too heavily, almost snorting in between sentences.* **Dan** *is very uncomfortable.*

**Graham**    Champagne is fucking awful.

**Dan**    Yeah.

**Graham**    Why would people bring champagne to a funeral?

**Dan**    I dunno.

**Graham**    There's a shitload in the kitchen. Help yourself if –

**Dan**    I'm all right. Thank you, though.

*Silence.*

Night then.

**Graham**    Wait!

*Silence as* **Dan** *stops.* **Graham** *looks at him for a while.* **Dan** *is unnerved.*

**Graham**    What did you do?

**Dan**    Eh?

**Graham**    You and Nick. What did you used to . . . do?

**Dan**    You know. Just – hung out. Listened to music.

**Graham**    I can't stop playing that record. Have you got any more?

**Dan**    Yeah.

**Graham**    The lyrics are incredible.

**Dan**    Yeah.

**Graham**    Do you want a drink?

**Dan**    I'm all right.

**Graham**    I could get you a beer if you prefer. Don't s'pose you like champagne?

**Dan**    No.

**Graham**    Did he like me, Dan?

**Dan**    Course.

**Graham**    I think he might have started to – started to find me out a bit. You know – there was that worship, that unconditional worship – I was the uncontested cleverest most athletic dad in the world . . . Do you think he thought I was . . . bit of a failure? Bottler? . . . Dickhead?

**Dan**   No.

**Graham**   He used to look at me like . . . (*Half-laugh.*) I am, you know . . . I'm all those things. I'm –

**Dan**   No.

**Graham**   I'm also fuckin' drunk.

*He laughs a little at first.* **Dan** *smiles.*

**Dan**   You were a bit scary.

**Graham**   You what?

**Dan**   Sometimes we knew to stay out of your way – when you came in –

**Graham**   Did you?

**Dan**   I –

**Graham**   He felt that, did he?

**Dan**   Only sometimes.

**Graham** (*looks* **Dan** *in the eye*)   I know you loved him too.

**Dan** *nods.*

**Graham**   Didn't you?

**Dan**   My best friend.

*Silence.*

**Graham** *lets out a roar.* **Dan** *looks terrified. He roars again, looks skywards.* **Dan** *begins to retreat.* **Graham** *looks at him.*

**Graham**   Don't – don't – don't go.

**Dan**   I'm –

**Graham**   Sorry. I didn't mean to –

**Dan**   All right.

**Graham**   I want to stand strong. You know? I want to be 'a man', Dan. Do you understand?

**Dan**   I think so.

**Graham**   But I ran away –

**Dan**   I don't think so.

**Graham**   He's my boy.

**Dan**   Yeah.

**Graham**   I keep going in his bedroom. (*Half-laugh. He looks at* **Dan**.) Is that one of his records?

**Dan**   Yeah.

**Dan** *hands him the record. It is the Melodians.*

**Graham**   They any good?

**Dan**   Yeah.

**Graham** *takes the record and removes it from the sleeve. He fingers the outside edge of the record with his index finger. Takes incredible care. He smells it. Takes cover of the record and fingers every millimetre of it. He puts the record to his face. Holds it in his hand.*

**Dan**   You're – you're spilling your drink, Mr –

**Graham**   Eh?

**Dan**   You're spilling your –

**Graham**   Graham. (*Emphatically.*) You must call me Graham.

*He looks at drink spilled all over himself, half laughs.*

Fucking hell.

*He laughs more loudly now, unsettling* **Dan**.

**Graham**   Fucking hell! Look at the state of me.

**Dan**   You're all right.

**Graham**   You're a good boy, you are (*He points at* **Dan**.) You're a good –

*He pulls* **Dan** *in close to his body, kisses the top of his head firmly. Smooths down the hair on his head clumsily. They stay there for a time.*

\*

**Graham** *moves inside with the bottle of champagne. The swing is raised.* **Dan** *moves to the record player and appears to be preparing a record. He takes off his shirt. Looks down at his bottle. Tenses his stomach. His chest. Smooths a hand over his chest and stomach, fiddles with his hair. He checks the record in the player. Removes his shoes and socks. He undoes his trousers and then loses courage and does them back up again. He puts his shirt back on.* **Marion** *enters in her nightgown.*

**Marion**    You can't stop smiling, can you?

**Dan**    No.

**Marion**    This doesn't mean anything.

**Dan**    I know.

**Marion**    It just means you're staying, nothing more.

**Dan**    I know.

**Marion**    I just wanted some company.

**Dan**    To stay the night –

**Marion**    Look . . . he's in Swansea until twelve tomorrow, but you have to be gone by nine, got it?

**Dan**    Why?

**Marion**    First thing, right?

**Dan**    Is he all right?

**Marion**    Graham?

**Dan**    He's . . . scary.

**Marion**    Did he say something to you?

**Dan**    Didn't say anything. He's just –

**Marion**    What?

**Dan**    I don't think he's very well. He needs help or –

**Marion**    Hey – hey – don't panic. Hey – love.

*She goes to him She smooths his hair down onto his head. She kisses him on the lips briefly, softly. He clings to her. Takes the air out of her a little. He stands back.*

**Dan**    The idea that I get to stay with you. Sleep in your bed. See you when you wake.

**Marion**    I wouldn't look forward to that too much if I were you.

**Dan**    I can't wait to see your naked skin.

**Marion** (*giggles in spite of herself*)    You are a funny one.

**Dan**    What? Is that wrong?

**Marion**    No, love, just . . . It's just you.

**Dan** *stands grinning at* **Marion**.

**Marion**    Maybe you should go at seven, you never know with Hayley's mum.

**Dan**    I can't get my breath around you.

**Marion**    Dan –

**Dan**    I can never get my breath.

**Dan** *takes his shirt off, stares at her intently.* **Marion** *is drawn to him but wary of letting herself go towards him.*

**Marion**    Dan . . .

**Dan**    I see your face everywhere, even when I close my eyes. I see your face on a dirty window on a train, hoisted up on brick walls, in pavement ponds and . . . I'd never hurt you . . . never.

**Marion**    Do you know what you're saying?

**Dan**    Yes.

*He takes off his trousers, is standing in just his boxer shorts.* **Marion** *tries not to look at him.*

**Marion**    Love is what's left when all of that sort of . . . dies. When you see the ordinary in everything and it doesn't frighten you any more and . . . When you can't feel the blood flying through you . . . When you can catch your breath . . . Am I making sense?

**Dan**    I do love you, Marion.

**Marion**    Do you?

**Dan**    I know what I'm saying. I do. Look at me.

*He smiles at her.* **Marion** *smiles.*

**Dan** *removes his watch, approaches her, goes to take her face in his hands.*

**Dan**    I've dreamed of this moment, Marion, for –

**Marion** *grabs his hands, holds his eye contact. Speaks with deliberate urgency.*

**Marion**    Don't you see I can't be the one to make the move here. I need to know that it's not just me. I'm dizzy here and God only knows what I'm doing but I – I can't feel like I'm coming after you – I can't pursue you, because it would be wrong. I need to know I'm not doing something wrong, Dan. I –

**Dan**    It's not just you. I came to you, remember.

**Marion** (*emphatic*)    I need you to understand, Dan. This isn't just . . . You know the risk for me is huge. All I have left I could lose if ever . . . I'm taking a huge risk for you. A huge risk. I need you to understand, Dan . . . You will be gentle with me? Cos I can't go back . . . after this. I can't –

**Dan**    Stop talking.

*He puts the needle on the record and moves into position to sing – this is prepared. The record is playing the Melodians' 'It's My Delight'. He sings.*

**Marion** *holds out her arms.*

**Marion**    Kiss my wrists.

*He does.*

\*

**Dan** *collects his clothes and goes to leave. He turns and beams a smile at* **Marion**. *Exits.* **Marion** *puts her robe on and sits opposite* **Louise** *at the table. She is watching* **Louise** *eat her breakfast.* **Marion** *looks at her own wrists. She rubs them, leans her forehead against them. Smiles.*

**Louise**    Are you in a mood?

**Marion**    Eh?

**Louise**    You're not listening, Mum.

**Marion**    I'm sorry.

**Louise**    It's wrong to abstain, you know?

**Marion**    What?

**Louise**    That's what the loony doctor at school says. 'It's wrong to abstain from grief because it's part of life.'

**Marion**    What did she say that for?

**Louise**    Cos I wouldn't go swimming.

**Marion**    I thought you liked swimming?

**Louise**    I was on my period.

**Marion**    Oh.

**Louise**    I'm not telling Mr Herbert that –

**Marion**    Lou –

**Louise**    He bloody freaks out.

**Marion**    I bet he does.

**Louise**    Maybe you should go and see the loony doctor, Mum? If you're sad?

**Marion**    I'm fine love. I'm –

**Louise**    They think I'm going mental cos my brother died.

*Silence.* **Marion** *looks at* **Louise** *but doesn't respond.*

**Louise**    I'm not mental.

**Marion**    No, love.

**Louise**    Do you get fanny gallops, Mum?

**Marion**   I beg your pardon?

**Louise**   Hayley says she gets fanny gallops all the time. When she sees someone she likes –

**Marion**   What?

**Louise**   Or sometimes if she sits on the washing machine she gets a bit . . . she says she gets a fanny gallop. A sort of . . . a pulsing in her fanny.

**Marion**   A fanny gallop?

**Louise**   I sat on the washing machine but it wasn't very comfy. Do you get them, Mum?

**Marion**   I . . . I think Hayley might be telling you stories again.

**Louise**   Do you get them when you're having sex?

**Marion**   Lou, I –

**Louise**   Do you?

**Marion**   You can talk to me . . . about . . . anything you like . . . Because your body does change and . . . if there's anything you'd like to talk to me about –

**Louise** *shrugs*.

**Marion**   – you can ask me, love.

**Louise**   Can Dan come for dinner tomorrow, Mum?

**Marion**   If he wants to.

**Louise**   I don't like veggie sausages, they taste like old parsnips and feet.

**Marion** (*laughs*)   You could have had toast for breakfast.

**Louise**   If you don't want me to be a vegetarian I could manage chicken – or fish fingers. I quite like fish fingers as long as you have enough ketchup.

*

**Louise** *leaves.* **Dan** *enters at speed. He pushes* **Marion** *onto the wooden dining table. Moves in to kiss her. Pulls her to the floor.*

**Dan**    Don't laugh.

*Stands back.*

**Marion**    I'm not laughing at . . . I'm happy.

*Silence. They look at one another. He smiles, she giggles a little.*

**Dan**    Did it feel like our bodies melted into one another?

**Marion** (*smiles*)    Yes, love, it did.

**Dan**    Yeah?

**Marion**    You did really well.

**Dan**    Good. Good – I'm glad.

**Marion**    It was wonderful.

*They giggle. She stands.*

**Dan**    Will you put your hand on my stomach?

**Marion**    Of course I will.

*She does.*

**Dan**    Feels nice.

*He lifts her top and feels her stomach. He giggles.*

**Marion**    Lou will be home soon.

**Dan**    We've got another hour.

**Marion**    We can't.

**Dan**    Just five more minutes, please.

**Marion**    Dan.

**Dan** (*looks like a wounded puppy*)    Please.

**Marion** *kisses his head. Giggles a little.*

**Dan** (*sings*)    'I love you like I want you, I kiss you like I need you, every night.'

**Marion** (*beaming*)   Come here, you beautiful boy. You beautiful, beautiful boy.

**Dan**   Can I kiss your neck?

**Marion**   You don't have to ask.

*He kisses her on the side of the neck and then holds her so she is standing still. He walks behind her.*

What are you doing?

**Dan**   Don't talk.

**Dan** *lifts her hair away from the back of her neck and smells her hair. Begins to kiss her gently.*

**Marion**   That feels wonderful

**Dan** *stops and stands in front of* **Marion**. *Holds her and pulls her in close to his body. She leans into him. He turns her round to face him. He holds her face. Kisses her.*

**Dan**   I give my heart to you.

**Marion**   I know.

**Dan** (*gazes into her eyes*)   I want to be part of your life, Marion.

\*

**Marion** *and* **Dan** *exit.* **Graham** *carefully prepares the table for dinner. He is meticulous in his preparations. He finally places a lit candle in the centre of the table.* **Marion** *enters with a dress half on. The zip is open at the back.*

**Marion**   Would you help me with this? (*Her dress.*)

**Graham**   I've got food on my – (*Shows her his hands.*)

**Marion**   Oh.

**Graham**   No . . . I – I can. (*Wipes his hands on his trousers.*)

**Marion**   Don't –

**Graham**   'S all right. Come here.

*He does up her zip. She flinches a little as he touches her back.*

What?

**Marion**    Nothing.

**Graham** (*turns her round*)    What?

**Marion**    Nothing. Tickles.

**Graham** (*unconvinced*)    Right.

*Silence.* **Graham** *pours them both a drink. They stand. Awkward.*

**Marion**    Are you sure you –

**Graham**    What?

**Marion**    Work tomorrow.

**Graham**    I might have a day off.

**Marion**    It's just that –

**Graham**    What?

**Marion**    Lou heard you last night.

*This stops him.*

Heard you screaming in the garden.

**Graham**    Right. What did you tell her?

**Marion**    Said you weren't feeling well.

**Graham** (*sarcastic*)    Yeah. I had a cold.

*Silence.* **Graham** *offers* **Marion** *a chair.*

**Graham**    I love you. Very much.

**Marion** (*kisses him on the cheek*)    And I love you.

**Graham** (*smiles*)    Then talk to me . . . Tell me anything – tell me where you are . . . Tell me what you're up to – how you're doing.

**Marion** *retreats a little.*

**Graham**    I miss him.

**Marion**    –

**Graham**    I said I miss him.

**Marion**    I know.

**Graham** (*half-laugh*)    I thought I could block it out, you know? I thought I could just be strong without . . . Am I making any sense?

**Marion**    I don't know what you . . . I don't know.

*Silence. She goes to take her glass.* **Graham** *grabs her by the wrist. He slams his other fist on the table five times very deliberately. Lets her go.* **Marion** *is frozen.*

**Graham**    You just – What is it, Marion? What am I – What is it?!

**Graham** *pushes* **Marion** *onto the table. Kisses her passionately. Holds on to her for a long time. The two of them lie there as* **Graham** *recovers his breath.* **Marion** *slowly slides away from him. Lights fall on the table as* **Marion** *wanders over to the garden. She stands alone, breathes deeply in and out. She smells the air.* **Dan** *approaches behind her. He tries to be quiet but she hears him. She doesn't turn round. Giggles a little.*

\*

**Dan**    Close your eyes again.

**Marion**    What are you doing?

**Dan**    I'm going to cradle you.

**Marion** (*laughs*)    You're what?

**Dan**    Close your eyes.

*She does, giggles a little.*

Spread your arms out wide.

**Marion**    Do what?

**Dan** *moves behind her and spreads her arms out wide. She giggles. He moves back a couple of paces.*

**Dan**    Now fall backwards.

**Marion**    I'm not doing that.

**Dan**    I promise I won't let you fall.

**Marion**    I dunno. (*She lets her arms fall.*)

**Dan**    Come on! Spread your arms out wide again!

*She stays there for some time before falling back into* **Dan**'s *arms. They laugh.*

**Marion**    That was lovely. Do it again.

\*

**Dan** *moves away.* **Marion** *begins to undress to her underclothes. She spreads her arms out wide.* **Louise** *enters,* **Marion** *jumps a little.* **Louise** *is wearing her pyjamas and holding a blanket.*

**Marion**    What are you doing up?

**Louise**    I can't sleep, Mum.

**Marion**    What's the matter?

**Louise**    I can't sleep.

**Marion**    Have you been getting nightmares, love?

**Louise** *nods and moves into the arms of* **Marion**.

\*

**Dan** *enters behind* **Marion**. *He undresses her very carefully. She is in her nightgown. She kneels in front of him. He begins washing her hair. He has a jug of water and pours it over* **Marion**'s *head. Strokes her clean hair. Puts her dressing gown around her. He moves her hair away from her neck at the back. Kisses her neck tenderly. She smiles. As he moves away she rubs her neck in pleasure.*

\*

**Marion** *and* **Louise** *move off. The windows of the kitchen have been covered in dark sheets.* **Dan** *enters and lights some candles. Prepares the scene. After a short time* **Marion** *enters. She smiles as she surveys the scene.*

**Marion**   It's lovely.

**Dan**   Really?

**Marion**   You're mad.

**Dan**   It took me ages.

**Marion**   Where did you get all the cloth from?

**Dan**   It's my mum's bedlinen.

**Marion** *laughs.*

**Dan**   I wanted us to have a candlelit dinner.

**Marion**   At two o'clock in the afternoon.

**Dan**   You have to use your imagination. Look – it's dark outside. I'll even paint a moon on one of the sheets if you like.

**Marion**   It's perfect, love. I can't see my food, but it's perfect.

**Dan**   I'll get some more candles.

*He goes to get up.*

**Marion**   No, no. Stay where you are.

*Silence. They look at one another.* **Dan** *leans across and grabs* **Marion** *by the wrists. He kisses them gently. She closes her eyes.*

**Dan**   I want to stay here, Marion.

**Marion** *smiles.*

**Dan**   I want time to stay where it is.

**Marion** (*flattered*)   Dan –

**Dan** *jumps up suddenly.*

**Dan**   Wait! I forgot. One more thing.

*He goes to the record player and puts on a record: 'Oh Baby', by Marcia Griffiths. It is played a little too loud. He dances a little as he comes back towards* **Marion**.

**Dan**    This one's for you. I found some Marcia for you.

**Marion**    What's it –

**Dan**    You're what I think of when I wake up in the morning. When I go to bed.

**Marion**    You are lovely.

**Dan**    I've been thinking we could go away.

**Marion** (*smiles*)    Really?

**Dan**    I was going to go travelling. I thought we could go travelling together. It would be amazing.

**Marion**    Dan.

**Dan**    Wouldn't it though? We could walk the edge of the world together. Be where there is no one else. It would be extraordinary.

**Marion**    Let's just –

**Dan**    Think about it. Tell me at least you'll think about it. I think it could be just what you need.

**Marion** (*laughs*)    All right, love.

**Dan**    I want to stand on my chair, spread my arms out and scream that I . . .

*He stands on his chair.*

**Marion**    Get down.

**Dan**    I love you, Marion . . . I love you.

**Marion** *laughs.*

**Marion**    Will you get down?

**Dan**    I do, though.

**Marion**    I know.

*He sits down.*

**Dan**   I made some dessert too.

**Marion**   Did you?

**Marion** *comes round and sits on his lap. She strokes his face, kisses his neck, rests her head on his shoulder.* **Marion** *can smell something. Her head jerks up and her face changes. She looks terrified.*

**Marion**   What are you wearing?

**Dan**   I'm sorry. I was going to get dressed up, but I look like an idiot in one of Dad's old suits.

**Marion** (*leans back*)   That jumper.

**Dan**   I wanted to be smart, I'm sorry.

**Marion** (*growing hysterical*)   I can smell it!

**Dan**   I'll change it then.

**Marion**   It's Nick's jumper.

**Dan**   I know.

**Marion** (*hurt, soft, childlike*)   Why are you wearing it?

**Dan**   I – You gave it to me.

**Marion** (*growing angry*)   I didn't think you'd wear it!

**Dan**   Marion.

**Marion**   Why would you do that? Why?

**Dan**   I'm sorry.

**Marion**   Why would you do that? Why! Why! Why!

*Gets off him.*

**Dan**   I like wearing it . . . I didn't think that –

**Marion**   Are you trying to hurt me?

**Dan**   Come on, don't, Mar—

**Marion**   Take it off.

**Dan**    What?

**Marion** (*hysterical*)    Take it off, take it off, take if off!

**Dan**    All right.

**Marion**    Take it off!

*She pulls at the jumper as he tries to remove it. She is very rough with him.*

**Marion**    Quickly.

**Dan**    You're hurting me.

*She pulls the jumper off and throws it to the floor.*

Calm down.

*She runs to the record player and turns the music off.*

**Marion**    I will not! I will not –

*She begins pulling down the sheets from the windows. The light pours into the kitchen.*

**Dan**    Marion, please, I didn't –

**Marion** *pulls the tablecloth and the food crashes to the floor.*

**Dan**    I never meant to –

**Marion**    Get out!

*She sits on the floor with her head in her hands, she cradles the jumper.*

**Dan**    Marion, please. How can I know? How can I know that . . . I'm sorry . . . Marion?

*He stands back from her, frightened to go to her.*

Marion? . . . Marion? . . . Marion? . . . I'll . . . Marion?

**Marion**    Just go, please. I need to be on my . . . Go please, Dan.

**Dan**    I want to make sure you're . . .

**Marion** *sits, shaking her head repeatedly.*

**Dan**    I'm so . . . Are you all right? What are you –

**Marion**    –

**Dan** *looks to* **Marion** *who will not look up.*

**Dan**    Marion?

**Marion** *stops. She sees* **Louise** *in the doorway. Looks at her.* **Dan** *does not notice* **Louise** *at first.*

**Dan**    Marion, are you –

**Louise**    What are you doing?

**Marion**    Nothing, love, I'm –

*She is huddled in a ball, protecting herself.*

**Louise** (*to* **Dan**)    What have you done to her?

**Dan**    Nothing.

**Louise**    Why's she crying then?

**Dan**    I haven't –

**Louise**    Mum? Mum? Are you all right?

**Marion**, *still curled up, shakes her head.*

**Louise**    You should go.

*She goes to her mother, holds her.* **Marion** *clings to her.*

**Dan**    What?

**Louise**    Get out!

**Dan**    Lou – I –

**Louise**    Look what you've done! Get out, I said!

**Dan** *looks to* **Marion** *who will not look up.*

**Dan**    Marion?

**Marion**    –

**Louise**    I'm going to scream. I swear. I'm going to scream.

**Dan**    Marion? I didn't mean to . . . Marion?

**Louise** Go.

*She screams.*

\*

**Dan** *is alone in his room. He paces a little. He turns on some music on his portable stereo. He listens for a while. After a short time he covers his ears. He hits the stereo off, pulls the CD out of the player and breaks it in half. He takes one of the records from the pile, pulls it from the sleeve and gouges his finger nails across it. He throws the sleeve and snaps the record in two. Does the same with another record. And another. He kicks the pile of records across the floor. He is out of breath. Crouches to the ground, holding himself.*

\*

**Louise** *and* **Marion** *are sitting at the table.* **Marion** *wears a dressing gown.* **Louise** *is in her school uniform.* **Marion** *is staring at the plate of food in front of her.* **Louise** *is watching. Waiting. There is silence for some time.*

**Louise** You should probably have something to eat. I could do you a jacket potato. And some beans. Gas mark 4 for an hour and beans on the hob until they start to bubble.

Mum?

Mum?

You do like jacket potato? I could grate some cheese on it too? Or . . .

Dad will be home, Mum.

**Marion** *pushes her drink away.*

**Louise** You can't stay like this. He'll start to worry. You don't want him to see you like this, do you? No one likes Dan at school. They think he's a bloody weirdo.

It's his fault, Mum.

**Marion** *shakes her head.*

**Louise**    Nick just felt sorry for him.

**Marion** *looks at her.*

**Louise**    I hate him, Mum.

**Marion** *looks away.*

**Louise**    I made you something, Mum. I drew it for you at school. Look –

*She hands her mother the drawing.*

That's you. That's Dad. That's Nick. Those are his angels.

**Marion**    –

**Louise**    I'm a bit old for drawings, I think.

**Marion** *shakes her head.*

**Louise**    That's my last one.

**Marion**    Love –

**Louise**    Do you like it?

**Marion** *struggles to hold herself.*

**Louise**    I talk to Nick every day still. I know he thought I was a bit of an idiot and I shouted at him but – but I still miss him.

*This floors* **Marion**.

**Marion**    Do you?

**Louise**    Course.

*Long silence.* **Marion** *is restless.* **Louise** *waits for her to speak.*

**Marion**    Will you do something for me, love?

**Louise**    What is it?

**Marion**    I want you to ask Dan –

**Louise**    No.

**Marion**    Please, Lou – Just need to see him –

**Louise**    I don't want to.

**Marion**    Please, darling.

**Louise**    No.

**Marion**    I need to speak to him −

**Louise**    Mum −

**Marion**    Will you ask him to meet me? Tomorrow?

**Louise**    Why?

**Marion**    I just need to see him −

**Louise** (*upset*)    Mum −

**Marion**    Just to sort things out −

**Louise**    Will you stop being sad if I do?

**Marion** (*nods, as much to herself as* **Louise**)    Yes, love.

**Louise**    You don't like him, do you, Mum?

**Marion**    Just need to see him −

**Louise**    You love me . . . You don't love him −

**Marion**    Please? For your mum?

**Louise** *stares at her mother. She searches her face. She is heartbroken.*

**Louise**    I'm embarrassed by you. Really I am. Look at you. How old are you? You're about fifty, aren't you? You're a mess. Look at the way you dress. I'd never look like that at your age. You've got no money. You work in a shitty job and you've let yourself go. I'd never be like that at fifty. What have you done with yourself? You're . . . cheap. Your clothes are horrible and you don't know how to put make-up on. You look awful. You shouldn't cheat on someone cos it totally destroys their faith in life, you know. I'd leave you. When I hear Dad crying in the bathroom at night when he gets back from the pub I think you did that to him. You must be hurting him. Not Nick. You. It must be you.

\*

**Marion** *sits at the table as* **Graham** *and* **Louise** *enter and begin to re-lay the table for breakfast.* **Graham** *lets the light back in and opens the windows while* **Louise** *carefully continues to prepare the table.*

**Graham** (*to* **Marion**)    Sorry I was late last night, love. Last time.

**Marion** *does not respond.* **Louise** *is looking straight at* **Marion**.

**Graham** (*to* **Louise**)    Have you got your bag?

**Louise**    By the door.

**Graham**    Eat up. Dan will be here soon.

**Louise**    Can't I walk on my own?

**Graham**    What's the matter with you?

**Louise**    Nothing. I just want to go early.

**Graham**    I'll take you now if you want?

**Louise** (*looks at her mother*)    You going to work tonight, Mum?

**Marion**    No, love.

**Louise**    Right.

**Graham**    I'll help you with your maths when I get in, Lou – if you like?

**Louise**    Thanks, Dad.

**Graham**    You're gonna kill those exams.

**Dan** *enters with his school bag.*

**Graham**    Hello, mate. She's nearly ready.

**Louise**    Hello. Daniel.

**Dan**    Hi.

**Graham**    Oh! (*Enthusiastic.*) I've got something for you, mate.

**Dan**    What is it?

**Graham**    Wait here –

**Louise**    Dad – we've got to go.

**Graham**    Two secs.

*He exits hurriedly.* **Marion** *dares not look towards* **Dan** *as* **Louise** *continues to watch her.*

**Louise** (*to* **Dan**)    You got your first exam today?

**Dan**    Yeah.

**Marion**    What exam is it?

**Dan**    Geography.

**Louise**    I hope you fuck it up.

**Marion**    Lou –

**Louise**    What?

*After a short silence* **Graham** *re-enters with a plastic bag in his hand. It has a record in it. He hands it to* **Dan**.

**Graham** (*with great enthusiasm*)    Here.

**Dan**    What is it?

**Dan** *pulls the record out of the bag.*

**Graham**    Limited edition 'Dekker'. White label '73.

**Dan**    I don't know what to –

**Graham**    I found it in the store on Oakfield. Amazing place.

**Dan** (*unsure*)    Thank you.

**Graham**    I knew you'd like it.

**Dan**    It's really kind of you.

**Louise**    It is.

**Graham**    It's a good-luck. For today.

**Dan**    It's just an AS.

**Graham**    Hope it goes really well.

**Louise** (*to* **Marion**)    Are you going to wish Dan good luck, Mum?

**Marion**    Good luck, Dan.

**Graham**    You should come for dinner later. We can celebrate –

**Dan**    I dunno –

**Graham**    Not celebrate, but – You could play your new record?

**Louise**    That would be nice.

**Dan**    Thank you.

**Graham** *hugs* **Dan**.

**Graham**    Good luck.

**Louise**    Are you gonna give Dan a hug too, Mum?

**Marion** *gets up slowly and hugs* **Dan**.

**Marion**    Good luck.

**Louise**    Bye, Dad.

**Graham**    Bye, love.

**Louise** *rushes towards* **Graham** *and hugs him. He is surprised, pleased. She turns towards* **Dan** *without looking at her mother and leaves.*

**Graham**    See you tonight.

**Dan**    Bye.

**Graham**    Don't be late.

\*

**Dan** *is in his bedroom. He sits against the wall. He begins to dress himself in smart clothes. Puts a shirt on and some trousers, then pulls the shirt off in frustration. He sits back on the floor.*

\*

**Louise** *begins to ready herself for a night out. She wears a short skirt and a low-cut top. It looks very wrong and awkward. She applies make-*

*up to her face. She puts on far too much eye make-up and begins to apply some lipstick.*

*

**Graham** *enters his bedroom as if he has come in from work. He removes his work clothing and changes into something more casual. He sucks his stomach in a little, preens his hair. Smoothes his hair down onto his head.*

*

**Marion** *looks at herself in a full-length mirror. She puts on the dress from the funeral. She presses it and tugs at it, trying to get rid of some of the remaining stains. She plays with her hair and straightens her necklace proudly. Looks at herself for a time.*

*

*The table is laid by* **Graham**. *He lays four places. As he is finishing,* **Marion** *and* **Dan** *take their seats separately. They do not acknowledge one another.*

**Graham**    How did you get on?

**Dan** (*shrugs*)    Dunno.

**Graham**    It went brilliantly didn't it?

**Dan**    I –

**Graham**    You stormed it.

**Dan**    Nah.

**Graham**    I bet you did. (*To* **Marion**.) I bet he stormed it.

**Dan**    Went OK.

**Graham**    We should have a drink – while we're waiting for madam.

**Dan**    OK.

**Graham** *exits to get some wine.*

**Dan** (*smiles at* **Marion**)    Are you all right?

**Marion** *looks through him.*

**Dan**    Are you all right? . . . Say something. Please? . . .
Marion.

*He reaches across the table to grab her hands. Stops himself.*

**Dan**    You're scaring me Marion. Please?

**Marion**    He knows.

*Silence*

**Dan**    What?

**Marion**

**Dan**    What did you say? Marion? . . . He . . . ? What? . . .
Marion?

**Graham** *re-enters with a bottle of wine.*

**Graham**    Look how beautiful Marion looks.

**Dan**    I –

**Graham**    Doesn't she? Dan?

**Dan**    You look very nice, Marion.

**Graham**    Looks amazing.

**Marion**    Thank you.

**Graham**    Everyone all dressed up. I even wore a shirt for
you. (*He smiles.*)

**Dan**    You look smart.

**Graham** (*pours some wine for* **Dan** *and* **Marion**)    I used to
hate speaking to anyone after exams. Everyone telling you all
the stuff you mucked up.

**Dan**    I just leave.

**Graham**    Very wise.

**Dan**    You can leave when you're done.

**Graham**    I bet there was a little boff asking for more paper the whole time –

**Dan**    Yeah –

**Graham**    Making you feel nervous –

**Dan**    Yeah.

*They laugh.*

**Graham** (*to* **Marion**)    Where is she?

**Marion** *shakes her head.*

**Graham**    She should be home.

**Dan**    Is she at Hayley's?

**Graham**    Yeah. But – I cooked.

**Dan**    Sure she won't be long.

**Graham**    She knew I was cooking.

**Dan**    Do you want me to go and get her?

**Graham**    No. You know what those girls are like.

**Dan**    Yeah.

**Graham**    Probably lost track of time. We can wait.

*Silence.*

What will you do?

**Dan** (*nervous*)    Eh?

**Graham** (*smiles*)    When you've finshed – A levels and –

**Dan**    I –

**Graham**    What will you do with your life?

**Dan**    I dunno –

**Graham**    So exciting –

**Dan**    I might travel.

**Graham**    Yeah? That sounds amazing. Doesn't it, Marion? Very exciting.

*Silence.* **Graham** *reaches across the table and takes* **Dan** *by the hand. He smiles at him.* **Dan** *begins to grow uncomfortable.*

**Graham**    Marion won't speak, Dan.

**Dan**

**Graham**    I said, my wife won't speak, Dan.

**Dan**

**Graham**    Not a word since yesterday morning.

**Dan**    Oh.

**Graham**    Have you noticed a change in her?

**Dan**    I – No.

**Graham**    When I came home last night she was . . . What's happened to her, Dan?

**Dan**    I –

**Graham**    How long have you –

**Dan**    I –

**Graham**    How long have you been sleeping with my wife?

**Marion** *gets up to leave.*

**Graham**    Where are you going?

**Marion** *looks at him.*

**Graham**    Don't go. Don't go now, love. We're only chatting.

*She leaves.* **Graham** *and* **Dan** *are seated at the table.* **Dan** *dare not speak. They sit there for some time.*

**Graham**    I don't know what's got into her. Did you break it off or something?

**Dan**    Please –

**Graham**   She looks like someone who's lost her son.

**Dan** *bows his head.*

**Graham**   I'm sure she'll be fine. You'll fix it. Won't you?

**Dan**   Please –

**Graham**   I hope you've prepared what you're going to say, Dan? To Marion? Will you say you're sorry? Will you say you will support her? Love her? What are you going to do, Dan?

**Dan**

**Graham**   Still, you look nice. Very well-groomed. That's the main thing.

*They sit there for a time.* **Graham** *looks at* **Dan** *who cannot hold eye contact.*

**Graham** (*stands*)   You can go up if you want.

**Dan**   I – But – I –

**Graham**   See Marion.

*Silence*

**Dan**   I'm –

**Graham**   What? What?

**Dan** *stands and retreats a little.*

**Graham**   I could pretend that I didn't know. When you're spending all this time here. When she won't let me near her any more. When she won't talk about her son. Our son.

**Dan**   I –

**Graham**   But you do know, I suppose. I knew.

**Dan**   Why didn't you –

**Graham**   She looked happy at times. Content even. I haven't seen her look like that for –

**Dan**   Mr –

**Graham**    Until last night. What did you do to her?

**Dan**    Nothing.

**Graham**    She looked like she was in a coma, Dan.

**Dan**    I –

**Graham**    Her soul has disappeared.

**Dan**    I – Mr –

**Graham**    You must call me Graham.

**Dan**    I – I . . .

**Graham**    You should go up. See her.

**Dan** *is on the edge of crying*

**Graham**    Go on. See Marion. Rescue her.

**Dan**    I dunno what you –

**Graham**    You should know she's been crying. For hours. She sits on the carpet and rocks back and forth. She looks like a fucking dizzy. Staring. Empty. Broken.

*Silence.*

She won't let me touch her. Maybe she'll let you. Touch her.

**Dan** *is shaking his head, retreating.*

**Graham**    No. Don't go, Dan. Don't go. Don't be scared of me. I'm not angry with you, Dan.

**Dan**    . . . Sorry.

**Graham**    Don't be sorry. Sorry for what? Does that mean you didn't mean to?

**Dan**    Yeah. Yeah – I – So sorry.

**Graham**    You didn't mean to sleep with my wife?

**Dan**    No. No – Sorry – Sorry.

**Graham**    Are you going to tell her that? Dan?

**Dan**    Sorry –

**Graham** (*bellows*)    You said that!

**Dan**    I – Why are you – I –

**Graham**    You're a man now, Dan. Men have courage. You have to be brave, Dan.

**Dan**    I didn't want to – I –

**Graham**    She's waiting, Dan. She needs you.

**Dan** *looks at* **Graham***. He begins to cry a little. He turns to leave. As he does so,* **Marion** *enters.*

**Graham**    Here she is, Dan.

**Dan**    Marion – Marion –

**Graham**    Speak to the boy, Marion. Say something –

**Louise** *enters.* **Marion** *looks at her. She is shocked.* **Graham** *and* **Dan** *are waiting for her to say something.*

**Marion**    Lou?

**Dan** *and* **Graham** *turn towards her.*

**Louise**    All right.

**Louise** *has eye make-up smeared down her face. She has badly applied lipstick which has been smeared across her mouth a little. She is dressed older than her years and looks a mess. She has been crying.*

**Graham**    Lou?

**Marion**    Louise?

**Louise**    Sorry I'm late.

**Graham** (*goes to her*)    Lou? Are you all right?

**Louise**    You should have started.

**Graham**    What's happened to you?

**Louise**    I've got a message for you, Daniel.

**Graham**   You've been crying –

**Dan**   Where were you after school?

**Graham**   What's happened, love?

**Louise**   Dan –

**Dan**   I waited for you.

**Louise**   Bunked off.

**Graham**   You did what?

**Dan** (*worried*)   Why?

*She shrugs her father off. Moves towards* **Dan** *and* **Marion**.

**Louise**   Couldn't be fucked. Fuck it all –

**Dan**   Lou?

**Graham**   What's going on?

**Louise**   My mum wants to meet you.

**Marion**   Lou –

**Louise**   Tonight.

**Dan**

**Louise**   She told me to tell you.

**Dan**   Don't –

**Louise**   Maybe she wants to have sex?

**Graham**   What's happened, love?

**Louise**   Do you have sex with her?

**Graham**   Louise –

**Louise** (*she faces* **Graham**)   I'm sorry, Dad –

**Graham**   What's the –

**Louise**   I'm sorry, Dad.

**Graham**   Lou?

**Louise** *goes to her father and hugs him. He doesn't move. She turns towards* **Dan**.

**Louise** (*glowers at* **Marion**)    It's disgusting –

**Dan**    No, Lou –

**Louise**    You're disgusting!

**Dan**    No –

**Louise**    I thought you were my friend.

**Dan**    I am –

**Louise**    I hate you. I fucking despise you!

*She sobs.* **Marion** *stands and goes to hold her.* **Marion** *spots a rip in her dress.*

**Marion**    Lou? Your clothes are ripped.

**Louise**

**Marion** (*worried*)    Lou – your clothes are ripped.

**Graham**    What have you done?

**Louise**    I went to Darren Feaney's house.

**Dan**    What?

**Louise**    That's where I went today.

**Dan** (*floored*)    No.

**Graham**    Who is –

**Louise**    And I kissed him.

**Dan**    Lou –

**Louise**    And I liked it –

**Dan**    You didn't –

**Louise**    And he touched me –

**Dan** *is on the verge of tears.*

**Louise**    And I liked it –

**Dan**   Tell me you didn't –

**Louise**   And I did – I did – I had sex with him. And I – I –
I – (*She is crying*) It didn't hurt. I wasn't terrified! He wasn't –
fucking – horrible – and –

*She goes to* **Dan**, *who stands.*

**Louise**   I hate you! I fucking hate you! You – you – you –
fucking – hate you!

*She hits him repeatedly with her open palm until she has run out of
breath. She looks at* **Marion** *and crumples into a chair.*

**Graham** *stands watching* **Dan**. *They stand there for some time.*
**Marion** *moves to* **Louise**, *who pushes her away.*

**Graham**   Who's Darren Feaney?

**Dan**

**Graham**   Who's Darren Feaney, Dan?

**Dan**   Boy at school.

**Graham**   What fucking boy at school!?

**Dan**   He's in her year. He –

**Graham**   He fucking – That's my daughter – that's my
daughter!

**Dan** *cowers.*

**Graham**   I can forgive almost anything, but harm to my
daughter I cannot.

*Silence.* **Louise** *has curled herself into a ball on the chair.*

**Graham** (*turns on* **Marion**)   What are you wearing? The
fucking pair of you –

**Marion**   I –

**Graham**   What are you doing, dressed up?

**Marion**   I wanted to.

**Graham**   For your meeting?

**Marion**    Love –

**Graham**    One of your walks? To think about Nick?

**Marion** *bows her head.*

**Graham**    Nick. Nick. Nick. Your son. Nick –

**Marion**    Stop it!

**Graham**    What did I say? Can you see him now? Can you, Marion? You remember your boy, Marion –

**Marion**    Shut – shut – shut – shut up!

**Dan**    You're scaring her –

**Graham**    You look silly, Marion.

**Marion**    I don't.

**Graham**    You look ugly.

**Marion**    Why would you –

**Graham**    Do you think she looks ugly, Dan?

**Dan**

**Graham**    How dare you! How fucking dare you!

**Marion**    Don't shout.

**Graham** *runs towards her and tears at her dress. She fights him off, but the dress is ripped.*

**Graham**    You look fucking ridiculous! You are fucking ridiculous!

**Marion**    My dress.

**Dan**    Mr –

**Graham**    You – you –

**Marion**    Stop it!

**Dan**    You're hurting her –

**Graham**    My daughter! My daughter! How could you?!

*He stands over* **Marion** *who crumples to the floor.*

**Graham**    Was it excitement?

**Marion**    Please –

**Graham**    Was it fucking –

*He is breathless, snorts a little as he tries to regain composure. He paces around* **Marion**, *who is rooted to the spot.*

**Graham**    Excitement is so cheap. So . . . passing. So fucking childish!

**Dan**    You're frightening her. You're –

**Graham**    It's sick, you know? It's repulsive. Disturbed. What's his mum going to think?

**Marion**    I don't know –

**Graham**    You're disturbed. You're –

**Marion** *puts her forearms over her ears.*

**Graham**    You'll hear this! You'll –

*He pulls her arms away from her face.* **Marion** *flinches.*

**Graham**    You've torn off my fucking skin, woman!

**Marion** *moves to leave.*

**Graham**    Where are you going? You'll hear this!

**Marion**    Please, love, I need to –

**Graham**    How would you – How could you –

**Marion**    Please, let me go.

**Dan**    Leave her –

**Graham** *turns towards* **Dan** *and paces toward him.* **Dan** *flinches.* **Graham** *points at the cowering* **Dan**, *but stops himself from touching him. He turns to look at* **Marion**, *who is trying to pull herself from the floor.*

**Graham**    Can't stay here now. Whole fucking street will –

*Silence.*

**Graham** (*calm*)   I could handle them avoiding me. Too bloody – to – I could handle the odd empty look of sympathy, the fucking 'I'm sorry's or 'if it were my' – I could handle that. But this –

**Marion**   Love –

**Graham**   We're a fucking freak show. You're a –

**Marion**   Love –

**Graham**   What have you done to my girl? What have you done?

*He is beginning to lose control again, walks aimlessly trying to gather himself. He sits on the floor with his legs crossed, searching for something to say.*

*Silence.*

**Marion** *again gets up to move. As she does so,* **Graham** *stands up, explodes with rage. He points at* **Marion.**

**Graham**   You! You've lost your right to grieve! Do you hear me? You've lost your right to grieve!

**Marion** *trembles on the ground.* **Dan** *is frozen to the spot.* **Graham** *moves slowly away from* **Marion.** *His breath is beginning to calm. After a time* **Marion** *lifts her head.*

**Marion** (*quiet, childlike*)   I love my son. God knows I love my son. (*Louder.*) More than – more than – I love my son. My Nicholas – my son – my son – my son. Don't you dare say that I – Cos I – love my boy.

*She rocks back and forth as she tries to compose herself.*

Don't take that away from me. You can't – Nicholas . . . Nicholas . . . Nicholas . . .

*She begins to cry. The crying is muffled into her body, but grows louder and louder. She is crouched over.* **Graham** *looks towards* **Dan,** *who still does not move. After a short time* **Marion** *stands, moves towards* **Louise** *and unravels her from her ball. She wipes her face with her* *hands and lifts her off the chair. She carries her off.* **Graham** *looks at* **Dan***, his eyes red and raw. He follows* **Marion** *and* **Louise** *off, leaving* **Dan** *alone.*

*

*Three weeks have passed.* **Marion**, **Graham** *and* **Louise** *are sitting round the breakfast table.* **Graham** *begins to tidy the breakfast things away as they are finishing. He puts some bits of food into a black bin bag. There is little left on the table. The room is empty.*

**Graham**    Have you got your case?

**Louise**    Yes.

**Graham** (*to* **Marion**)    Could you pass me the juice?

**Marion** (*passes him juice*)    Thanks for making breakfast.

**Graham**    That's all right.

**Marion**    It was lovely.

**Graham**    We should go as soon as he comes.

**Louise**    Why's he coming?

**Graham**    He's got some stuff of your brother's.

**Louise**    I don't want to see him.

**Graham**    Lou –

**Marion**    Only coming to say goodbye.

**Louise**    Well, he can fuck off.

**Graham**    Oi!

**Marion** (*ruffles* **Louise***'s hair*)    Come on, you.

**Graham**    Do you want to see the garden again?

**Louise**    Yeah.

**Graham** *passes* **Louise** *his phone. She looks at the picture.*

**Louise**    It's massive.

**Graham**   Picture doesn't do it justice, Lou. You wait.

**Marion**   It's beautiful.

**Graham** *kisses* **Marion** *tenderly.*

**Graham**   Finish your breakfast. (*To* **Louise**.) And go to the toilet, you.

*He exits.*

**Louise**   I don't want to go back to school.

**Marion**   You've got three more weeks' holiday.

**Louise**   I don't want to go though.

**Marion**   New school, love. New friends.

**Louise**   You don't just make new friends. I'm not three.

**Marion**   You might like it.

**Louise**   Yeah.

**Marion**   Might be great.

**Louise**   Will you brush my hair?

**Marion** (*pleased*)   If you want me to.

**Louise** *moves to* **Marion,** *hands her the brush.*

**Louise**   Not too hard.

**Marion**   I won't.

**Louise**   Dad does it too hard.

**Marion**   Does he?

**Louise**   He tries, but he's not very good.

**Marion** (*smiles*)   He likes doing it.

**Dan** *enters.* **Marion** *sees him. She stops brushing* **Louise**'s *hair. They both look at* **Dan***. He holds a stack of records. He waits a moment before speaking.*

**Dan**   Door was open.

**Marion**   Hello, Daniel.

**Dan**   Hi, Mrs Neill.

**Louise** *looks away.*

**Dan**   Hi, Lou.

**Marion**   Are those his records?

**Dan**   Yeah. I – I cleaned them.

**Marion** *goes to take them from him.*

**Marion**   Thank you.

**Graham** *re – enters with a suitcase.*

**Graham**   Hi, Dan.

**Dan**   Hello.

**Graham**   Thanks for bringing them over.

**Dan**   No problem.

**Graham**   Are you going to say goodbye to Dan, Lou?

**Louise**   No.

**Graham**   Go and wait in the car then.

**Louise**   Dad –

**Graham**   Go on.

**Louise** *looks at her father, then at* **Dan**. *She walks past* **Dan**.

**Dan**   Bye, Lou.

*She exits.*

**Graham**   Got your results yet?

**Dan**   Next week.

**Graham**   Good luck, yeah?

*He drops his case and offers his hand to* **Dan**. *They shake hands.*

**Dan**   Thank you, Mr Neill.

**Graham**    I do mean it, you know.

**Dan**    Thank you.

**Graham**    I'll see you in the car, Marion.

*He kisses* **Marion** *on the cheek. He picks up the case and walks out.*

*There is a long silence between* **Marion** *and* **Dan***. They look at one another for a long time.*

**Marion**    You should keep the music.

**Dan** *nods, tries to accept this.*

**Dan**    I don't want the music any more. I can't stand it.

**Marion**    I'm sorry to hear that.

**Dan**    And since . . . since . . . I really can't sleep now, Marion. I can't.

**Marion**    I'm sorry.

**Dan**    Marion –

**Marion**    Goodbye, Daniel.

**Dan** *stands and says nothing.* **Marion** *moves to leave. As she walks past him, she turns for one last look.* **Dan** *still has his eyes on her. They look at each other for a long time. She steps towards him.*

*Lights down.*